THE ADVENTURE OF KNOWING AND BEING KNOWN BY GOD

CHAD KARGER

LUCIDBOOKS

Go Outside

The Adventure of Knowing and Being Known by God

Copyright © 2017 by Chad Karger

Published by Lucid Books in Houston, TX
www.LucidBooksPublishing.com

All rights reserved. No part of this publication may be reproduced, stored in a retrieval system, or transmitted in any form by any means, electronic, mechanical, photocopy, recording, or otherwise, without the prior permission of the publisher, except as provided for by USA copyright law.

ISBN-10: 1632961571
ISBN-13: 9781632961570
eISBN-10: 163296158X
eISBN-13: 9781632961587

Scripture quotations are from The Holy Bible, English Standard Version® (ESV®), copyright © 2001 by Crossway, a publishing ministry of Good News Publishers. Used by permission. All rights reserved.

Special Sales: Most Lucid Books titles are available in special quantity discounts. Custom imprinting or excerpting can also be done to fit special needs. Contact Lucid Books at Info@LucidBooksPublishing.com.

Table of Contents

Introduction 1

Chapter 1: How Much More 9

Chapter 2: A Cramped Place 17

Chapter 3: A Broad Place 25

Chapter 4: The Isolation 35

Chapter 5: The Community 45

Chapter 6: The Consumer 57

Chapter 7: The Gardener 67

Chapter 8: Headed Home 79

Afterword: The Potter's Hands 89

Acknowledgments 95

Notes 99

Introduction

> You have to stalk everything. Everything scatters and gathers; everything comes and goes like a fish under a bridge.
>
> —Annie Dillard, *Pilgrim at Tinker Creek*

Have you ever been to Houston? Houston is a sprawling, concrete, unzoned, billboarded, beautiful mess! When I moved there as a college student, I never thought I'd stay for nearly 27 years. For all of its concrete and congestion, it became home to me and my family. My wife, Meeka, and I raised our three kids, forged the most important friendships of our lives, faced struggles, and experienced great joys there. In other words, our roots sank deep, and transformed an isolating and alienating city into a rich community. It was a place of knowing and being known. This kind of community slowed us down and cultivated and nourished our lives with God's grace.

For several years, I served at a church that was located in the shadow of downtown Houston skyscrapers. It was a newly planted church and we were renovating a decades-old church building. From the outside, the red brick building looked like a lot of churches built

Go Outside

during that period in Texas, complete with a gymnasium. And, like a lot of those churches, it was empty. Our shoestring budgets and limited experience were no match for the audacious vision we had for the corner of Taft and Drew. In addition to holding Sunday services in this vacated building, we imagined it becoming a hub of activity for our community. It was a crossroads that would foster relationships and engagement with our community. The dreary, vacated building's renovation was a physical demonstration of how the gospel brings renewal and hope. Its newly lit rooms were meant to speak about the light and life we have found in Jesus. That transformation turned out to be one of the most difficult undertakings I've ever been a part of. Much of the struggle was the result of our countless mistakes along the way!

Often, I would bring my mountain bike to the office. During my lunch hour, I'd hop on the bike and navigate the winding streets of East Montrose until I reached Buffalo Bayou. The green, rolling hills along the banks of the chocolate brown river water were where the urban landscape met the sliver of natural habitat. Dodging walkers and joggers, as well as cars and trucks, I'd race toward Memorial Park and turn a couple of loops in its densely wooded trails before heading back to Taft Street. The jaunts on my bicycle at lunch, and the gritty work of bringing to life an old church, opened my eyes to see the beauty of God in the sprawling city. For years I had worked in well-manicured environments, but this place seemed untamed and teeming with God's Spirit. The relatively small, underfunded, and passion-filled community was a part of bringing God's redeeming and renovating story to our city.

Now, why do I mention all of that to you? Inasmuch as this book is about walking in places like the one pictured on the cover, it is about God leading us further into the adventure of faith through the sacred and ordinary places of our lives. It's about knowing God

Introduction

and being known by God in spaces that are as familiar to us as they are often overlooked. It's a book about coming awake to God's powerful and abundant presence, and getting rid of the clutter that blocks our view of God's mercy offered to us in Jesus. It is about walking out of the small and cramped confines that sin has trapped us in and into the wide-open spaces where we revel in God's goodness and experience our deepest joys.

In his classic book *No Man Is an Island*, Thomas Merton writes, "One of the most important—and most neglected—elements in the beginnings of the interior life is the ability to respond to reality, to see the value and the beauty in ordinary things, to come alive to the splendor that is all around us in the creatures of God. We do not see these things because we have withdrawn from them."[1]

Believe me, in a city like Houston it is easy to withdraw, especially in the summer months! My bike rides during the lunch hour would usually require a shower immediately afterwards! But, Merton is getting at an emotional and spiritual withdrawal as well as a physical withdrawal. The natural course, as we will see later in this book, is to demand that life be as predictable and manageable as we deem necessary. This demand requires that we withdraw from the places where we have little to no control. A self-made world will eventually dull our innate, God-given sense of the Divine and Other, which is present all around us. Merton is challenging believers and spiritual seekers to go outside of the walls of predictable and manageable life and to engage the untamable, passionate, and creative God. As all-consuming and all-powerful as God is, Merton is pointing to the ordinary and familiar places where we find Him.

Faith, then, leads us outside! It is a life that begins with a stirring in our soul and eventually leads us outside of the safety and predictability of our homes and out of our hurting hearts. By God's grace in Jesus, our souls come to life and we are compelled to take

Go Outside

steps of faith. Out on that trail, our faith is further strengthened by the realization that God knows us and cares for us. He is found in the company of His children and in the work we do together. This, in turn, beckons us onward, further, and full of hope.

Encountering God requires faith. By God's grace through Jesus, we have access to God. Faith, then, is the action we take in response to God's initiative. Faith is the action we take in response to God's self-disclosure in Jesus. Faith is not blind, but requires instruction, knowledge, and necessitates action. A growing and vital faith leads us outside of ourselves and into something much larger and glorious than we ever imagined. It awakens us to the beauty all around us; it awakens a longing for something more without causing us to despair. One of my hopes for you as you read this book is that you'll be struck with sudden urges to go outside! To venture outside your front door or beyond the gate of your worries to find God's goodness and mercy.

Early Pioneers

Throughout the Bible, God's call to people of faith led them to action. The call of God doesn't lead to the life of a settler, but that of a pilgrim. This is what Hebrews 11 describes. Known as a sort of roll call of heroes in the faith, the writer describes people of faith who were uprooted, called out, and who journeyed by faith. Their journeys included uncertainty and undaunted courage, each step echoing with assurance and conviction. "Faith is the assurance of things hoped for, the conviction of things not seen" (Heb. 11:1).

Hope is the guiding vision that faith produces. Pilgrims carry that vision in their heart like a flame, a light from within lighting their path. It opens their eyes to God's presence at any given moment and leads them to the future hope of being at home with God. Pilgrims of faith confront struggles with honesty and joy, "groaning

Introduction

inwardly as they wait eagerly" (Rom. 8:23) for their "blessed hope" (Titus 2:13).

Not even death can quench the flame of hope. Those listed in Hebrews 11 died while moving faithfully through this life (Heb. 11:13). They only caught a glimpse of the things promised. But God is not disappointed in these faithful souls; he is pleased to be their God and has prepared a place for them (Heb. 11:16). Having parted from this world, their stories are now part of "the great cloud of witnesses" (Heb. 12:1), pointing us onward and further in pursuit of God's Kingdom. "Therefore…let us also lay aside every weight, and sin which clings so closely, and let us run with endurance the race that is set before us, looking to Jesus, the founder and perfecter of our faith, who for the joy that was set before him endured the cross, despising the shame, and is seated at the right hand of the throne of God" (Heb. 12:1–2).

We look to Jesus. The man born in Bethlehem is our "light and life" shining in the darkness before us (John 1:4–5). In Jesus, the promise of reconciliation with God is fulfilled. After Jesus departed this earth, he sent the Holy Spirit to be with us—friend, guide, and counselor (John 16). Every step of faith we now take is based upon the assurance that God is present and He will be faithful to His promise for salvation. Pilgrims of faith refuse to settle for the status quo or be dismayed by occasional doubts. Their faith is rugged and real as they journey with others, encouraging one another; their kingdom is both a future destination and a present reality.

Knowing and Being Known by God

This book is written for the pilgrim. In addition to this book awakening the urge to go explore right outside your door, my hope is that this book points you to the God-shaped areas of your life that by His grace reveals the practical places whereby to engage

Go Outside

Him on a daily basis. This is not as much about a sacred pilgrimage in a foreign land as it is recognizing the potential encounters with God's glory every day. For me, the truth and wisdom imparted to me in countless sermons and Bible studies have often come alive in the reality and practicality of everyday living, on my bicycle, and on the backpacking trail. Sometimes the best classroom has been the one without walls!

From May to October in Southeast Texas, the heat and humidity make the air feel like a warm bottle of syrup. As oppressive as the heat can be, however, the rest of the year includes countless days inviting us outside. Whether you live in a national forest or in a sprawling city, there are lessons to be learned and applied. Go explore the neighborhood. While sometimes we have to strain to see evidence of God's handiwork between the sprawling concrete jungles, we'll be surprised by what we find, and find ourselves singing with the Psalmist: "For you are great and do wondrous things; you alone are God" (Ps. 86:10).

There are aspects of God's character and power that aren't experienced in our manmade environments. Again, to see those aspects, you have to go outside—go asking, seeking, and knocking! For most people, spending time with God means sitting in a quiet room with their Bible and praying. While these are essential practices, these disciplines ought to move us to action!

The truth in the Bible opens our hearts to experience God at work all around us, whether in creation, in community, or in the satisfaction of hard work. The Word of God invigorates us and prayer is our direct line of communication with God: "Our Father in heaven, hallowed be Your Name; Your kingdom come, Your will be done on earth, as it is in heaven" (Matt. 6:9–10). Scripture reading and prayer work together to awaken us to "his eternal power and divine nature" (Rom. 1:20). Scripture reveals the true nature of

Introduction

the universe and our place therein! As the Psalm says, "Be still and know that I am God; 'I will be exalted among the nations, I will be exalted in the earth!' The Lord of hosts is with us; the God of Jacob is our fortress" (Ps. 46:10–11). Instead of making us sedentary, these disciplines enliven us for the adventure of faith. On that adventure, we come to see our humanity in light of God's majesty and glory, power, and sovereignty. We come to know that God has been there all along. He knows us better than we know ourselves:

> *O Lord, you have searched me and known me! You know when I sit down and when I rise up; you discern my thoughts from afar. You search out my path and my lying down and are acquainted with all my ways.*
>
> Ps. 139:1–3

Passages like this one aren't telling us how to get close to God. They are pointing to the fact that God is near to us—closer than we ever imagined! When we get trapped inside of routines and patterns that distract us from God's presence, it requires steps of faith to reengage the God who is powerfully and abundantly near. While that may require us to leave behind our comfort zones, we can be sure that God will not disappoint us, but will provoke awe and gratitude like what is found in the Psalms: "Praise him, sun and moon, praise him, all you shining stars! Praise him, you highest heavens, and you waters above the heavens!" (Ps. 148:3–4).

We are meant to sing with the sun and moon and stars! Our humanity flourishes when we are enjoying God's presence. This joy will come as we disrupt lifeless patterns and break from paths leading us to the same old deadends. Without these disruptions, the reality of God begins to fade into the background. As we lose sight of God, we, therefore, lose contact with our true calling and purpose as people made in God's image. We soon find ourselves feeling frustrated and defeated at every turn. What we need is to

Go Outside

go outside.

Much of this book has grown out of my work as a pastoral counselor and guide to people at various places on their journey. As much as they came to me for help, I experienced God's faithfulness in their struggles and in their victories. Their seeking and asking encouraged me to do likewise. I've also had the privilege of going for long walks in places like the one on the cover. These wild and untamed spaces are spectacular classrooms where God's beauty and power are on display. The fruit of countless conversations in the counseling office and on the backpacking trail converge in the following pages. I've had the privilege of seeing individuals take bold and courageous steps of faith in pursuit of God and His kingdom. When we are pilgrims and have yet to arrive home, we must share with each other evidence and stories of God's love and mercy, His presence. Thankfully, instead of straining to see Him in all of His holiness, God has come near to us in the person and work of Jesus. So, together, we fix our eyes on Him as we take the next step.

Chapter 1:
How Much More

> Bearing God's image is not a fact, it is a vocation. It means being called to reflect into the world the creative and redemptive love of God.
> —N.T. Wright, *The Challenge of Jesus*

Nearly 30 years ago, I went for my first backpacking trip. I spent eight days in the mountains near Taos, New Mexico, with a dozen other guys. My parents planned this trip for me seeing it as a good opportunity for me to reconnect with my faith. I was 16, and saw it as an adventure. Neither my parents nor I knew all the ways that God would use those days in the New Mexico wilderness.

My memories of that time are vivid. I recall the heavy external frame backpack and the winding trail through the forest. It took a couple of days before we reached the line in the forest where the trees begin to disappear making way for an exposed, wide-open view of our surroundings.

Along with fewer trees, the entire ecosystem changes above tree line. The dry, shallow soil is carpeted by rich alpine tundra. It is inhospitable to oxygen-dependent creatures like us humans. As rugged as it is, though, there are amazing flowers and grasses that

Go Outside

emerge when the snowpack melts. Spring lasts only a short time, maybe a couple of months at these altitudes in the Rocky Mountains. However, nature wastes no time putting on an outlandish display during that short amount of time.

As we emerged from the densely wooded forest, this amazing view opened before us. I had never felt so small in comparison to my immediate surroundings. Nor had I felt that removed from civilization. The slow and difficult ascent up the winding trail those first two days led us to a place of rest and rejuvenation, if not a little light-headed and exposed. The journey was all at once stunning and arduous. It was the rain, blisters, leaky tents, and food shortages. It was the combination of the beauty *and* the struggle, feeling small *and* alive that lingers in my memory. I learned a lot in the paradoxes of that trip.

I had grown up in the church. As a teenager, though, I had begun to lose interest in matters related to my faith. In all honesty, I began to feel increasing amounts of guilt and boredom. God was portrayed in very moralistic and predictable ways. The mystery of faith wasn't discussed. Questions, doubt, and difficulty were signs of weakness. No one talked much about daily struggles for those in the faith. The abundant life Jesus was offering looked drab and stale. Like most teenage boys, I saw friendships and athletic achievement as sources of happiness and satisfaction. My attention was easily diverted.

I wasn't so much a victim of fundamentalists as I was headstrong, egocentric, and, so I thought, indomitable. This wasn't my parents' fault or my pastor's fault. The stories of God seemed tame and inconsequential to my self-absorbed worldview. The challenge of my athletic pursuits and beautiful young ladies seemed like good substitutes for the incomparable, loving, wild God revealed in Scripture. Over time, these substitutes served only to annoy and

How Much More

irritate me as they weren't able to live up to that for which my heart longed—such as the artificiality of religion, where guilt is the primary motivator. So my selfish choices left me empty, insecure, and frustrated. It was about this time in my life that I took that walk in the woods. Those days in the wilderness energized me while at the same time humbled me in comparison to God's vast and beautiful creation. I was overcome and enlivened.

Boredom is a spiritual condition. It's also an epidemic in our online world. It seems like the logical result of being self-absorbed, wealthy, and dissatisfied. It is closely linked to frustration and, over time, rage. Before sending me on that backpacking trip, my parents were sensing the frustration and irritation that was coming out of me. They figured a grueling walk in the woods might be helpful.

God used those eight days to take me outside of my small, self-centered life and into His powerful and abundant presence. By His grace, it was more than an amazing walk in the pristine wilderness of New Mexico. A survey of the extraordinary handiwork of God in creation opened my eyes to the ordinary ways in which He is powerfully and abundantly near.

God subdued me on that trail; I was put in my place. I could feel that I was small, dependent, and weak in comparison to creation, much less the Creator! But being brought low resulted in a spiritual rejuvenation. Standing on the edge of my limitation and seeing the infinite power and mercy of God in creation brought comfort to my soul. His mercies in Jesus came into focus as my self-sufficiency faded from view. I could rest in the redemptive and reconciling power found in Christ alone.

The Good News in Jesus is that God has exerted His power and secured our rescue from sin and His wrath (Rom. 1:16–18). In

Go Outside

Christ we are saved from our rebellious and futile efforts to find life outside of the One who gave us life. We are given rest for our souls: "Come to me, all who labor and are heavy laden, and I will give you rest" (Matt. 11:28). Jesus's call loosens our grip on self-preservation so that we can take hold of him. It opens the door so that we can go outside and into His bountiful pasture: "For he is our God, and we are the people of his pasture, and the sheep of his hand" (Ps. 95:7). Where sin has made the world small and convinced us that self-reliance is the only way through life, Jesus invites us outside and gives us faith in God.

The gospel of Jesus leads us outside of our self-centered world and into the wide world of God's glory and pleasure. Jesus calls out to his disciples to enter into the care and providence of God. "Do not be anxious about your life." He goes on to say, "Look at the birds of the air: they neither sow nor reap nor gather in barns, and yet your heavenly Father feeds them." Then, later, "Consider the lilies of the field, how they grow: they neither toil nor spin, yet I tell you, even Solomon in all of his glory was not arrayed like one of these" (Matt. 6:25–26, 28–30).

The grass, birds, and flowers, as well as you and I, are dependent upon the Word of God. By the Word we are created and sustained. By the Word we are saved from sin and death. The Word of God is our only *hope*. For that reason, the Word took on the flesh of a first century Jewish carpenter. Jesus of Nazareth is the Christ, the Messiah, the Rescuer! He is our Liberating King, The Righteous One. He leads us *outside* of our worry and anxiety and *into* life as God designed.

A survey of the highest mountain or the smallest flower can be used by the Holy Spirit to remind us of God's power and abundance. Scripture is relentless in portraying these attributes of *God*. We, on the other hand, are *weak and poor*, our minds racing with and distracted by novelties and anxiety about falling behind. Into

How Much More

this darkness, Jesus's voice is a light directing our attention to creation in order to reveal the Creator, "Look at the birds of the air. Consider the lilies of the field, how they grow...will he not much more clothe you, O you of little faith?" (Matt. 6:26–30).

There's no way to connect with what Jesus is saying unless we take Him at His word: unless we go outside. We can't over spiritualize what Jesus is saying here. He wanted to draw His worried disciples' attention away from the source of their worry. Worry tunnels our vision. Faith widens the lens! And so Jesus instructed them to look at specific parts of creation. Birds, grass, and flowers in their natural habitat offered them pictures that lead to spiritual truths. But Jesus wasn't leaving them in a perpetual state of meditating on creation. Creation is there to lead us, with the guidance of God's Word in Christ, to God Himself!

God is nudging us outdoors, into fields and forests, so as to give us a better view of Himself and ourselves. Outside, in God's creation, the Holy Spirit directs our attention to God's caring and providential hand. Inside, it all depends on us. Outside, we take our place with God's other creations, totally depending upon His care. Inside, our imagination is dim. Outside, our hearts and minds are opened to God's reality. Inside, life is compulsive and addictive. Outside is the life of faith, hope, and love. Outside, the new life in Christ awaits. Outside, we live into the purpose for which we were created, "to glorify God and enjoy him forever" (Westminster Shorter Catechism, Question & Answer 1).

Similar to my walk in the woods when I was a teenager, Jesus's sermon in Matthew 6 leads the disciples to a realization of our limitations: "And which of you by being anxious can add a single hour to his span of life?" (Matt. 6:27). This is not a deadend of shame and self-loathing. Instead, the gospel reveals God's love and mercy in my weakness and sin.

Go Outside

"Are you not of more value than they?" (Matt. 6:26b). Jesus's question penetrates our hearts by grace and quickens us with faith so that we come awake to God's providence and care in our lives. When we stop fighting and cursing the one who came to help us, and instead embrace His love, a vision for real life, indeed abundant life, begins to take shape.

In the pages that follow, I want to explore this vision with you. The book is organized around three essential elements of our humanity. These aspects of our humanity are given to us by God and are restored by the work of Jesus.[2] The work of God's grace through Jesus restores worship, redeems relationships, and reshapes our stewardship.

Worship

You and I were made to worship. I first began to grapple with this in graduate school as I studied biblical counseling. I learned that to bring the Word of God to bear on people's souls in their time of need was to invite them to worship the One True God in the midst of life's struggles and joys. Conversely, counseling was the subtle, strategic, and intense effort to shine the light of the gospel on idolatrous strongholds in a person's soul. Instead of seeing worship as simply attending a Sunday service where the congregation sings hymns or praise songs, I hope you will come away knowing how this aspect of our humanity permeates everything we do in our lives. Two of the main theaters in which worship or, conversely, idolatry unfolds is in our *relationships* with each other and the *stewardship* (management) of our time, talents, and treasures.

Relationship

God created the man and put him to work, caring for the garden. But he was not to do this alone. So, God created a partner for Adam. In comparison to worship and stewardship, relationships

How Much More

are the place we experience some of life's richest joys and deepest heartaches. The effects of God's grace are most pronounced and the vandalism of sin is most treacherous in our relationships with each other. I want to explore both the brokenness in our relationships and God's promise of healing in our relationships. The healing we experience in relationships comes as a result of the healing in our relationship with God the Father. I hope that you will come away knowing that you are not alone, and knowing that you weren't meant to live in isolation. God's presence through his Holy Spirit is experienced in creation and in community.

Stewardship

Work is not a curse! Work was part of the plan for living in paradise! No sooner had Adam awakened from the dust with the breath of God in his lungs than he was employed by his Creator. God had made a beautiful place that was fruitful and teeming with life. He had shaped it from nothing by His powerful Word. It was very good! Having created Adam in the image of the Three-In-One God, the man was directed to oversee and cultivate the garden as God's cocreator and manager. Together, the man and woman would work and rest just as God had created them. But their disobedience changed their relationship with God, with each other, and with the work of their hands. Instead of joy, their work would be threatened by pain and futility. It is my hope that the final section of this book will renew a vision for the work God has given you to do, regardless of your vocation or personal affairs, with a new sense of purpose and meaning that glorifies God.

In the next chapter, we will begin our journey with the overarching mandate God has given to us planted deep in our soul. The mandate in which our desire for worship arises.

Chapter 2:
A Cramped Place

> The God before whom the believing soul is annihilated is also the one from whom strength and consolation are to be sought.
>
> —Merold Westphal, *God, Guilt, and Death*

You are here.

When I was a kid, I had a knack for getting lost. Disregarding my parents' instructions, I'd follow my curiosity until I got lost and needed help finding my way back. At the mall, for example, my parents would leave me in the toy store where I was to wait for them to return. Without fail, I would leave the store with no idea where my parents were shopping (these were simpler times of course!). I'd find the public information booth, let them know I couldn't find my parents, and take a seat while my parents responded to the public address system. Even if I was lost, I knew the grown-ups weren't!

Maybe this explains why I like maps so much. I like to know where I am at all times. I like to open the map app on my phone and watch the blue dot trail along while taking road trips. I like to use the "my location" button and the zoom out feature to get a sense of where

Go Outside

I've come from and how much farther I have to go until reaching my destination. However, as nice as phone mapping can be, topographical maps that are printed on real paper are a must-have on the backpacking trail. Instead of pushing a button, the hiker uses fixed points and a compass to determine his or her current location. Still, the key to finding your way, whether on a road trip or out on the trail, is knowing where you are, your current position.

This is the problem with sin in our lives. It distorts our understanding of our location relative to God. The sinful mindset wrongfully assumes that finding my way begins with me. In many ways, finding my way begins, as it did in those malls when I was a child, calling out for help. Finding my way means calling out to God and being found in Jesus. This calling and waiting, however, is counterintuitive to the sin-stained heart and mind. Despite what we think, we are desperately lost. In Romans 1, Paul tells us that God gives us what we want as an act of judgment on our sin: "And since they did not see fit to acknowledge God, *God gave them up* to a debased mind to do what ought not to be done" (Rom. 1:28, emphasis added).

"God gave them up" is a chilling and colossal statement. Every parent who has ever had a child hell-bent on making destructive choices has a sense of what this statement means. Sometimes the hardest and most loving thing you can do is let your son or daughter carry through with their choices in hopes of seeing them repent. This may mean watching your kid hit rock bottom in an addiction or a failed relationship. But a wise parent knows that true repentance only comes after truly seeing the futility of your own way and, by God's grace, turning to Jesus. This parent-child relationship is in view in Romans 1, as Paul describes God's relationship with fallen humanity. Having turned our backs on the truth, we have turned to face life on our terms, apart from God.

In Genesis 3, Moses tells the story of how the serpent convinc-

A Cramped Place

es Eve that God is withholding from her what her heart really desires and deserves. She is convinced that the good she wants will come by taking matters into her own hands. The serpent subtly plants a seed of doubt in her mind with regard to God's goodness and truthfulness: "Did God actually say…" (Gen. 3:1b). Can you hear that? I imagine someone rolling their eyes and sighing as they say, "Did God actually say *that*? Seriously!"

As the conversation progresses, she sees the fruit in a way that she has never seen it before. The serpent has convinced her that right there, hanging on the tree, is fruit that is good for food, is beautiful to look at, and will provide wisdom.

Food. Beauty. Wisdom.

She feels a growl coming from somewhere deeper than her stomach. The hunger is coming from her soul. "This is what I want! This is what I deserve! And God is standing in my way! Here, Adam, let's eat this!"

No sooner is the fruit juice trickling down their throats than "the eyes of both were opened and they knew that they were naked" (Gen. 3:7). Chances are you have read this verse before. Or, you have heard someone read it. But, have you ever stopped to think about what just happened? This is like a bomb being detonated in the middle of the garden, in the hearts of these two people. More than that, it's the first of countless detonations for generations to come. And, yet, it's so easy to miss. *The seed of doubt concerning God's goodness grew into the poison fruit of self-centeredness, self-help, and self-condemnation.* The garden didn't go up in flames. The creatures weren't suddenly possessed by demons. Adam and Eve didn't start attacking one another. And Satan didn't suddenly appear in human form. It's like a bomb went off in the deepest ocean and a tsunami rushed toward land. The tidal wave washed them into hiding and shame, fear and worry. Everything changed. She saw the fruit on the tree differently before she ate it; and, having eaten the fruit, now they both saw themselves as shameful and weak. But there's more.

"And they sewed fig leaves together and made themselves loincloths" (Gen. 3:7b). Not only were their worlds rearranged around this newfound self-awareness, but they were busy with a cover-up. They immediately tried to hide what they now considered to be their hapless and pathetic selves.

Just about the time they finished with their fig leaves, they heard something that was familiar and yet different; the sound of God in the garden. The sound that used to be welcomed with joy became a terror, so they hid. The fig leaves were intended to keep them safe from each other. The garden's foliage and shadows were used to hide from God. Self-centeredness gave way to self-help, which gave way to self-loathing. Ever since Adam and Eve, we, their children, want nothing to do with God.

"But the Lord God called to the man" (Gen. 3:9). This is a ray of hope in an otherwise dark and frightening place. Instead of leaving them to their devices and ridding himself of them, God calls to them, "Where are you?" It's a sign of grace and mercy when Adam and Eve were expecting something they had never considered before that point: hostility. God's question broke down the hostility and invited them to respond in truth. And respond they did.

"I heard the sound of you in the garden and I was afraid, because I was naked, and I hid myself" (Gen. 3:10). Again, Adam had never felt panic when the sound of God's presence was near. This new way of sensing and reacting to the world put him on edge. He was afraid for his life. There was confusion and chaos. Moreover, he essentially told God, "I was afraid because I was so shamefully naked and you were near." He took matters into his own hands. Self-preservation

A Cramped Place

kicked in just as automatically as he was breathing and his heart was beating. Forget about Eve, Adam ran for cover. Sin, as it turns out, makes the world much smaller for mankind. Instead of expanding our horizons, sin chases us into a prison of our own making. Adam was hiding out, no longer living in and enjoying the garden, but instead was playing it safe. And God wouldn't stand for this.

God drew them out of their hiding place and they immediately knew what had happened. They had disobeyed God. Instead of the beauty and peace of paradise, they chose self-determination. They took matters into their own hands. Upon further questioning, Adam blames Eve and God: "The woman whom you gave to be with me, she gave me the fruit of the tree, and I ate" (Gen. 3:12). When God turns to Eve, she blames the serpent (Gen. 3:13). Not only does sin turn us inward, it makes us defensive against others. It plants the lie of helplessness in our minds. We become convinced that while we may have made a mistake or two, there are many more people to blame.

Regardless of this unbelief, God drew near. While He did pronounce judgment, God also announced plans for salvation. Out of His infinite mercy, God removed their self-made coverings. In its place, God made coverings and clothed them. He dressed their wounds like a father would his child, even though the child is at fault. He cared for them. He saved them.

Surely, when God called out, "Where are you?" it wasn't because God had been duped. Rather, God's question was an opportunity for Adam and Eve to confess. It was a chance to step back into the light and, cringing, be exposed by the light of God's grace and truth. God drew them out of their self-made predicament. He rescued them from enemies too strong for their ever-shrinking place of isolation and into a broad and beautiful place of community. Why did God do all of this? *God delighted in them.*

Go Outside

Psalm 18:16–19 describes this same rescue operation, just much later in the story. It is David's perspective of salvation.

> *He sent from on high, he took me;*
> *he drew me out of many waters.*
> *He rescued me from my strong enemy*
> *and from those who hated me,*
> *for they were too mighty for me.*
> *They confronted me in the day of my calamity,*
> *but the Lord was my support.*
> *He brought me out into a broad place;*
> *he rescued me, because he delighted in me.*
>
> Ps. 18:16–19

Here's the good news: our absurd, weak, and naked selves are not enough to make God run away from us. God's holiness includes a bottomless delight in us, His image-bearing creatures. The revelation of his glorious delight most certainly includes the recognition of our absurdity. In Isaiah 46, God, through the prophet Isaiah, calls out to his rebellious children of Israel, who trusted in idols, saying: "To whom will you liken me and make me equal, and compare me, that we may be alike?" They lift it to their shoulders, they carry it, they set it in its place, and it stands there; it cannot move from its place. "*If one cries to it, it does not answer or save him from his trouble*" (Isa. 46:5, 7, emphasis added).

In other words, God says, "How are those fig leaves working for you? How are those self-made replacements, which are your burdens, helping out?" Idolatry, Tim Keller says in his book *Counterfeit Gods*, is ascribing good things with ultimate and absolute status. This is what Paul says we are all doing since that implosion in the garden. "For although they knew God, they did not honor him as God or give thanks to him, but they became futile in their thinking, and their foolish hearts were darkened" (Rom. 1:21).

A Cramped Place

We have become futile in our thinking. Instead of wisdom, we have worry. Instead of beauty, we have shame. Instead of sustenance we are panicked and fighting for survival. We are exactly where we never thought we'd end up. We are in a world of our own making and it is closing in around us. The seeds of our destruction are sown and we have no hope for salvation. Our constant efforts to cover up and pretend are threadbare and continually mock us.

But the Lord calls to us, "Where are you?" By those gracious words we are found. While God gave us up to our sinful choices, *He didn't give up on us but sent Jesus to rescue us.*

Chapter 3:
A Broad Place

> Amazing grace! how sweet the sound,
> That saved a wretch; like me!
> I once was lost, but now am found,
> Was blind, but now I see.
>
> —John Newton

I recently traveled to New York City for the first time in my life. My friends and I navigated the streets like hobbits who had wandered far from the Shire! Of its hustle and bustle there seems to be no end. My eyes could barely take it all in, my head swiveling like a toy being drawn to the brightest, loudest, and most peculiar sights. Masses of people everywhere were moving swiftly, as if carried along by an invisible river. There were noises coming out of the concrete, steel, and glass, a constant bombardment of not-so-subtle messages to buy and consume more of this, that, and all of it! In short, I loved it! But I was also glad I was only there for a day and a half!

We stepped out of the glare of Times Square into a small theater on Broadway. We had tickets to the musical *Amazing Grace*, the story of John Newton, the slave trader turned pastor. He wrote the hymn by the same name and was instrumental in abolishing slavery in the United Kingdom.

By the end of the musical, I had all but forgotten that I was in New York City. Transported with the rest of the audience to the 1700s, we all stood with the cast at the climax of the musical to sing with one voice, *"Amazing grace, how sweet the sound that saved a wretch like me; I once was lost, but now I'm found, was blind, but now I see."* It truly was amazing.

We exited the theater like congregants dismissed from church, deeply moved by the power of that confession and God's grace, which saved a man whose greedy and ruthless heart seemed beyond reach. With little time to absorb the power of this story, we were ushered out the doors and back into the reality of New York City. The sweet sound of grace echoed in our hearts and minds while people were moving, going, searching, begging, and buying.

Grace is a powerful, other-worldly force. Grace is the power of God for salvation (Rom. 1:16). Grace rescues and reorients us. Instead of leaving us firmly at the center of our world, God's grace is like an earthquake that rearranges the very ground upon which we stand. This is what God's grace did to John Newton and to Jacob.

Jacob's Ladder

From the opening chapter in Scripture, the story of God's relationship with men and women is at the forefront. Male and female, they are created in the image of God and are the recipients of God's powerful and abundant presence at every turn. Even when Adam and Eve rejected God's plans in favor of their own, God came looking for them and rescued them. Where there is judgment, as in Noah's story, there is a gracious promise. Eventually

A Broad Place

God's invasive love and grace finds Abram and Sarai, an unknown and unexceptional couple. After decades of walking with God by faith, the promise of a child is fulfilled, Isaac.

Of all the characters in the Bible, Isaac's son, Jacob, is one of the most perplexing. To start with, he is born to a woman who had been barren and unable to conceive. His conception was the answer to his father's prayer. In fact, God gave Isaac and Rebekah twins. Jacob shared Rebekah's womb with his twin brother, Esau. From the time they were conceived until late in their adult life, the Bible says they were at odds with one another.

We are introduced to the young men in Genesis 25. It is a story about exploitation, extortion, and misaligned priorities. Esau trades his birthright to Jacob for stew and bread. It is pretty clear that Esau had little regard for the gift of his birthright; Jacob, on the other hand, wasn't beneath exploiting his brother's hunger in order to take hold of this priceless possession.

The very next story about these brothers involves deception with the help of Rebekah (Gen. 27). Isaac is all but blind and asks Esau, his favorite son, to hunt for and prepare his favorite dinner, which would be one of the last meals Isaac would share with his son Esau. Rebekah overhears Isaac's request and, because Jacob is her favorite, she calls Jacob and conspires with him to trick her husband. Once Rebekah and Jacob had prepared a feast and dressed the boy in his brother's clothes, Jacob comes to Isaac's bedside. Jacob convinces his father that he is his brother. Then, Isaac says, "Come near and kiss me, my son," and with that Isaac blesses Jacob (Gen. 27:26–29).

No sooner had Jacob left the room in possession of his father's blessing and his brother's birthright, then Esau enters. Isaac immediately realizes what has happened and trembles with rage (Gen.

27:33). Esau is enraged, too, and says in effect that Jacob has lived up to his name, which in Hebrew means cheater. "Now Esau hated Jacob because of the blessing with which his father had blessed him…" and after his father's death, Esau vows to kill his brother (Gen. 27:41).

Jacob, with his mother's help and urging, packs his bags and runs for his life, quite literally! Having left home, instructed by Rebekah to find a wife in his Uncle Laban's household, Jacob comes to a nameless place and lies down to rest. With his head on a rock, he dreams of a ladder that reaches to heaven (Gen. 28:11–17). Angels are going up and down on it and the Lord stands at the top of the ladder. Jacob hears the voice of the Lord say to him, "I am the Lord, the God of Abraham your father and the God of Isaac. The land on which you lie I will give to you and to your offspring" (Gen. 28:13). God promised Jacob countless generations of children who will be found in every corner of the earth and, through whom, all the people of the earth will be blessed. "Behold," the Lord continues, "I am with you and will keep you wherever you go" (Gen. 28:15).

With that, Jacob awakens and exclaims, "Surely the Lord is in this place, and I did not know it" (Gen. 28:16). *Nor did Jacob know ahead of time or do anything to earn God's love.* Before he was born, the apostle Paul points out that God declared, through the prophet Malachi, "Jacob I loved, but Esau I hated" (Rom. 9:13).

Not only is this declaration significant as it relates to God's sovereign plan unfolding in the life of Abraham, Isaac, and Jacob, but also because of what it means for the life of Jacob. Loved by God, Jacob awakens from this dream having received a promise from the Lord that Jacob would never be alone as he walked in the promise of God. Jacob also embarks on a long and difficult journey that would come to a head on the night before he is reunited with

A Broad Place

Esau. By that point, Jacob has wives and children and extraordinary wealth. He has endured the ironic trickery of his father-in-law and found himself face-to-face with his twin brother, Esau, who all those years earlier vowed to kill him. From the time they both leave home to the point that they are reunited, the Bible is all but silent concerning Esau (Gen. 29–32). It's as if in fulfillment of the prophecy spoken about these boys ("Jacob I loved, Esau I hated."), God has left Esau to himself and to amass wealth. But, Jacob has struggled from one step to the next, all the while increasing his wealth. From this, we learn that to be loved by God means to struggle with God and with God's promises. *To be hated by God is to be left alone, to wander without purpose. To be loved is to be written into God's story by His grace; to be hated is to be left out.*

The story of Jacob's early life comes to a climax on the edge of a river named Jabbok. As he dreads the reality before him, he prays and recalls the promise God made to him that very first night he had left home (Gen. 32:9–12). After he prays, he plans for the reunion the next morning. After he plans, he forges the river and finds solitude on the opposite side of his family and possessions. He is alone, so he thinks. That night, the Bible says a "man wrestled with him until the breaking of day" (Gen. 32:24). Whereas the first night from home Jacob was reassured by a dream of God's blessing, this night, of all nights, was full of restless struggle. He wrestled with God. Instead of being destroyed by God, he receives a blessing. But, this is no ordinary blessing! It is a blessing that hurts. It is grace that leaves Jacob limping. And, it comes with a new name.

Jacob had begged the man to identify himself. But, instead, the man renames Jacob. "Your name shall no longer be Jacob, but Israel, for you have striven with God and with men, and have prevailed" (Gen. 32:28). As is the case with all the names in the Bible, this one holds special meaning, as it would be the name of those generations God had promised Abraham, Isaac, and Jacob. The name, Israel, denotes God's struggle with and for His people. He had loved Jacob and struggled with him, all the way to wrestling with him. He would love the people of Israel and struggle with them, all the way to crucifying His son, Jesus, on the cross. But, instead of being destroyed in that struggle, God would save His people. He would save Jacob's life and bless his life. Through the death and resurrection of Jesus, God would save His people throughout the earth.

Jacob's encounter with God on the eve of his most dreaded hour resulted in a limp. Instead of it being a curse, the limp, for all of its pain, was a blessing. And so it is with God's grace for all who by faith take hold of it: grace can take a curse and turn it into a blessing. Grace is a force that will not leave us alone. It reorients and restores, and it renames us as those who are loved by God. By God's grace we are all brought into the family who trace their heritage back to Jacob. Once named for his cheating ways, by grace Jacob becomes known as one for whom God had struggled in order to save. Incredibly, at the end of his life, Jacob, now Israel, upon meeting the Pharaoh of Egypt, says that his life has been relatively short and difficult. Then, with those words, he reaches out to bless the Pharaoh in the name of the Lord (Gen. 47:9–10).

A New View

The Bible is God's story about the struggle to save His people and all of His creation. There are countless characters, some of whom seem, at times, to be struggling against God. Saul, who would come to be known as Paul the Apostle, is a prime example. Not unlike Jacob's struggle with God, Saul meets Jesus on the road to Damascus (Acts 9). While Saul doesn't wrestle with God, as Jacob did, he comes away with a different sort of limp: blindness!

A Broad Place

Through this overpowering encounter with God's grace, Saul becomes Paul and becomes God's chosen missionary to the nations. Of all of his letters, which he wrote to churches he once sought to destroy, the letter to the church in Rome stands out as one of the most important.

In the first 11 chapters, Paul lays out the gospel of Jesus Christ. In the very first chapter he boldly and unapologetically exclaims, "I'm not ashamed of the gospel, for it is the power of God for salvation" (Rom. 1:16). From there, the mercenary-turned-missionary writes the most comprehensive summary of what God has been doing since Genesis 3, when he found Adam and Eve hiding with their fig leaves. He tells the story of Jesus, the One through whom salvation has come to all by grace through faith (Rom. 3:23–24). Paul then connects the dots from Jacob's ladder to Jesus on the cross. God has been faithfully and graciously relentless in the story of salvation stretching all the way back to Adam and Eve, extended in Noah, and straightway through Abraham, Isaac, and Jacob. When we consider its scope and depth, it is hard to find another single passage in the whole of the Bible that depicts God's merciful grace as revealed in and through Jesus. It's a passage that all who follow Jesus should pay close attention to.

God's grace, as described in Romans 1–11, is not mere spiritual abstraction. This grace, again, reorients our lives around and in light of God's love. In the final verses of chapter 11, when Paul surveys all that has been revealed to him and through this letter, he is left speechless…well almost. In Romans 11:33, Paul begins his benediction with one simple word, "Oh." He is, as it were, silenced by what God has done and continues to do. The view of God's mercies has left him struggling to find the words that are up for the task of praising and giving thanks to God. With the guidance of the Holy Spirit, Paul has moved this letter from *woe* (Rom. 7:24) to *oh*!

Go Outside

From, "No one is righteous, no, not one" (Rom. 3:10), to "There is therefore now no condemnation for those who are in Christ Jesus" (Rom. 8:1), to, finally, "If you confess with your mouth that Jesus is Lord and believe in your heart that God raised him from the dead, you will be saved" (Rom. 10:9). And, having been saved, the only logical, rational, reasonable response is worship:

> *Oh, the depth of the riches and wisdom and knowledge of God! How unsearchable are his judgments and how inscrutable his ways! "For who has known the mind of the Lord, or who has been his counselor? Or who has given a gift to him that he might be repaid?" For from him and through him and to him are all things. To him be glory forever. Amen.*
>
> Rom. 11:33–36

God's grace in and through Jesus restores worship, one of the essential features of our humanity. Thus, Paul's appeal to the church in Romans 12:1–2:

> *I appeal to you therefore, brothers, by the mercies of God, to present your bodies as a living sacrifice, holy and acceptable to God, which is your spiritual worship. Do not be conformed to this world, but be transformed by the renewal of your mind, that by testing you may discern what is the will of God, what is good and acceptable and perfect.*

Paul appeals to the church in Rome and to all of Jesus's followers, to do the only thing that makes sense once they have surveyed the mercies of God: "present your bodies as living sacrifices." Far from a lifeless, robotic life of faith, *worship is living and sacrificial. It is the response born out of awe and gratitude. It is more than Sunday morning sing-alongs and begins in earnest once the Sunday service ends. It is the whole life response to what God has done in and through Jesus.* Worship, in other words, is obedience. Instead of obligation, obedience is the grateful response of Jesus's followers.

A Broad Place

Furthermore, worship has very practical, everyday implications in our lives. As we grow in our gratitude for what God has done, our minds are transformed. We are enabled to discern God's very good, acceptable, and perfect will. The question for Christ's followers is not, "What Would Jesus Do?" The real question that inspires a life of worship is, "What Has Jesus Done?" To this we say, or, in response to God's grace and love, we join the chorus of the Psalms, both in word and deed: "My soul longs, yes, faints for the courts of the Lord; my heart and flesh sing for joy to the living God" (Ps. 84:2).

The rest of Paul's letter to Rome explores the practical implications of the life of worship. It will center around two main areas that we will explore in the rest of this book. First, it will touch on our *relationship* with others, especially among the family of God—the church. Secondly, it will explore *stewardship*, the renewed call to be God's cocreators and managers of our time, talents, and treasures.

Out of the depths of self-centered preoccupation with our shame and brokenness, God draws our attention to a much larger and beautiful world. Paul says in Romans 12:3, "For by the grace given to me, I say to everyone among you not to think of himself more highly than he ought to think, but to think with sober judgment, each according to the measure of faith that God has assigned."

The sweet sounds of God's amazing grace in our lives result in God-glorifying rhythms in our relationships and in our stewardship. As the old hymn proclaims, *"Twas grace that taught my heart to fear, And grace my fears relieved; How precious did that grace appear. The hour I first believed"* ("Amazing Grace," John Newton, 1779).

We all have to see our need for God's grace. Grace is our covering. Far from an added boost to our self-help projects, grace is a gift of God that brings real hope.

Chapter 4:
The Isolation

> To do its worst, evil needs to look its best.
> —Cornelius Plantinga, Jr,
> *Not the Way It's Supposed to Be*

Signs of the fall are everywhere.

As I write, we are in the midst of one of the most disappointing presidential election cycles that I can remember in my lifetime. Grown men take the stage to debate what the citizens of this country hope to be substantive issues of public policy and interest. Instead, candidates sound like delinquent and belligerent school boys. The more I listen, the more complicit I feel I become in their foolishness. Everyone loses when we see each other as objects either useful for advancing our cause or obstacles impeding our progress. This is true in presidential elections, marriages, and churches alike. This is what happens, however, when we see each other as competitors instead of companions, and life as a zero-sum game in which the winner takes all.

For most of us, these candidates are characters in a spectacle far removed from our daily lives; they can be turned off with the push of a button—yet, we can't look away! Signs of the fall and the division between people can be found much closer to home. If not in our churches, then we need not look any further than our families. We see signs of people using others to get advancements and promotions at work. Or we may see an old friend on Facebook and feel the swirl of resentment and envy for their happiness and good fortune.

The speed of our busy lives certainly doesn't help in forging meaningful connections with other people. We have neglected time to linger with each other, especially since we are competing against one another. Moreover, people slow us down. We speed ahead all the while lying to ourselves that quality is more important than quantity when it comes to time spent with others we love. German theologian, Jürgen Moltmann, captures this predicament well: "The modern man has a great many encounters, but does not really experience anything, since although he wants to see everything; he internalizes nothing and reflects upon nothing. He has a great many contacts but no relationships, since he is unable to linger because he is always in a hurry. Only the person who lives slowly gets more out of life!"[3]

Eyes Wide Open
The serpent told Eve that she would see the world differently once she ate the forbidden fruit. The snake accused God of wanting to keep her in the dark. Lies always come with promises and this one was no different: the knowledge of good and evil. The world as you know it, the serpent hinted, will expand with your newfound knowledge. You'll be like God.

Their eyes were opened. Their perspective and knowledge, however, contracted. They became self-conscious of their frailty and vulnerability. The world collapsed into a consuming self-aware-

The Isolation

ness. Instead of the absence of shame, now they were hiding from each other. They were separated from each other. Instead of enjoying each other's company without insecurity, they now saw the other person as something to avoid. Instead of seeing another person created in the image of God, they saw an object standing in the way of what they wanted. As one writer, Martin Buber, observed, in a fallen world I see an it and not the person who is my companion. "There are many ways of living in the world without You."[4] In this way, the objectification of others is a destructive and vandalizing force at work in God's creation.

The garden became a cemetery.

Their companion became the adversary.

God became their enemy.

If sin has vandalized[5] worship, turning it into idolatry, then it has also vandalized relationships leaving us alienated. Not only are we alienated from each other and from God, but we are alienated from ourselves, too. The fact that we are consumed with ourselves and yet alienated from ourselves is a tragic and tortuous irony in our sin. To be sure, our adversarial relationship with others is in part rooted in our adversarial relationship with ourselves.

Bargain Basement
Meeka and I had been married three years when we moved to Denver.[6] We didn't have much money, but we had a lot of time. On the weekends we liked to find hiking trails to explore. One day, we hiked to the top of the shortest mountain above 14K feet in elevation in Colorado. While we sat on the peak under a clear, blue sky, I convinced her that we could make another summit if we went down a different direction. The only catch, we had to hike across a trail called Sawtooth Ridge. The ominous-sounding passage led

to the adjoining peak. Thankfully, my wife is adventurous. There wasn't a lot of arm-twisting going on that day. But, to be sure, what we did next was all my idea.

We weren't a hundred steps onto the ridge when the peril of this trail became all too apparent to us. To the left was a sheer cliff that fell hundreds of feet to the meadow below. On our right was a cascading pile of sharp, dry, and clumsy boulders leading to an alpine lake. The scree, as it is called, seemed to be our safer option. So we started to balance on the sharp angles of the rocks as we made our way down the ridge's southeast side. As we did, I could tell that she was nervous and unsure. That frustrated me. It was like we were having a conversation with each other without speaking a word! Her eyes burrowed into the back of my head as she wondered why she had listened to me.

Suddenly, she lost her footing and fell. A jagged edge of the boulder scraped her leg. The injury wasn't serious, but it hurt. I helped her to her feet again and, like the tough and brave woman she is, she continued to follow me as we made our way farther down. I could feel this terrible and, again, frustrated, irritation growing in me. At the time, I wasn't sure of why I felt irritated. But I did. I was also feeling increasingly insecure about my abilities to lead us. *What have I done? How do I get us out of this place? I've led her out here and she's scraped up her leg and is frustrated. I ruined the day. She thinks I'm an idiot.*

As I listened to the voice in my head, not paying much attention to her, I became convinced that I needed to assert myself and gain the upper hand. I needed to show her, and the world and myself, that I knew what I was doing. Without a second thought, I challenged Meeka's concern, "Don't you trust me?"

Without hesitation, she snapped back, "No! I don't trust you. But,

The Isolation

right now I don't have a choice."

What a stupid question. What an even better response! It's not one I have soon forgotten all these years later. Let me be clear, that wasn't the last time I have acted and sounded like a self-centered fool in our 27 plus years of marriage! As God has often done in our relationship, He has addressed my foolishness through my wife's love and strength. Over time, I could see that on the side of the mountain that day I was trying to manipulate Meeka into reassuring me. Instead of thinking about her and caring for her, I was passive-aggressively (maybe not so passive!) trying to get her to make me feel better about myself. She was the one who had fallen and scraped her leg! My lack of empathy was all too apparent and directly related to my bruised ego. In my twisted, self-centered mind, her making me feel better about myself was way more important than me being kind and gentle in our struggle on the mountain.

Instead of drawing near to her in that moment, I was hiding. I was alienated from what would really make me happy and was alienating her and her needs. In other words, I was using her. I was treating her like an object instead of relating to her as the person God had made her to be. This way of relating cheapens relationships and people. It's easy and cheap, not deep and authentic. With time and help, through biblical counseling, I came to see myself in that moment looking for a bargain. I wanted just enough relationship from Meeka to get my ego stroked; but, I didn't want to get so close as to have my insecurity exposed. I wanted the largest amount of relationship at the smallest possible cost to me. Instead of seeing her as my ally, I saw her as my adversary. This is what happens in marriages, churches, and presidential politics when sin runs unchecked.

Go Outside

Below the Waves

Over the years, the more I've learned about God's salvation in Jesus, the more I've learned about how cold and manipulative my heart can be. Having made progress and matured by God's grace, I still find myself diving back into old, fearful patterns. My wife and my three kids have learned a lot about Jesus in my shortcomings and weaknesses. I've also been disappointed and hurt in relationships. The hurt can give way to unchecked anger. Sometimes the anger seems to be pointed at myself; at other times I feel the anger in me is directed toward others. Unchecked, anger closes me off from God's grace and leads me to a defensive posture. Living on the waves of my anger makes life about mere survival. By God's grace, the Holy Spirit directs me below the anger and into the heart of my disappointment. Here's where I groan and wait and long for God's healing. It is here that I'm opened up to His mercy and healing. As Paul says in Romans 8: 23, "[I] groan inwardly as [I] wait eagerly" for God to complete the work of salvation He has started in me. The sooner I can be honest about my hurt and disappointment with others, the sooner healing can begin.

Don't get me wrong—anger is a valid emotion. There are legitimate reasons to be angry in this world. Some of them are very personal and injurious. Unexplored, however, anger can wreck our lives. Anger is like the waves of an angry sea that eventually overwhelm our lives and take us under. What needs to happen is we must shift to the source of our anger. Angry people are defensive; hurting people are vulnerable. If we can identify the hurt that is fueling our anger, we are in a position to meet Jesus and experience the healing of His grace. This, however, requires us to be honest about how our hopes have been dashed in relationships. It requires us to identify our disappointments. We have to be honest about desires that grew from longings that were planted in our soul by the Creator. Being vulnerable when we are disappointed is an invitation to take part

The Isolation

in the work God is doing in us and in others. Being vulnerable is worth the risk when it comes to God's movement in us and through us. This is at least in part what Paul meant when he confessed: "Therefore I will boast all the more gladly of my weaknesses, so that the power of Christ may rest upon me" (2 Cor. 12:9).

Where Are You?
Instead of giving them completely over to their fig-leaf existence, God comes looking for Adam and Eve in Genesis 3. Whereas once the couple looked forward to hearing the sound of God moving through the garden, now, having disobeyed God, they are afraid. In fear, they attempt to do the impossible: hide from God!

"Where are you?" (Gen. 3:9). That question leads us all the way to Jesus, the Word of God who took on the flesh of our humanity and drew near to us in our weaknesses. Jesus is the embodiment of "Where are you?" Jesus's life was the light shining in the darkness and "the darkness has not overcome it" (John 1:5). Despite all of the hurt and anger that has us hiding and defending, God comes looking for us in Christ Jesus. The Bible is full of stories of God finding people in the shadows of their own poor decisions or the abuse of others. Whatever the cause, grace is extended to the groaning and waiting. Still, to this day, God is calling for the lost sheep. But as was the case with Adam, and even in parts of the Bible, those needing rescue weren't always sure how to respond. *Their fear competed with their faith.*

"I heard the sound of you in the garden and I was afraid," Adam confessed. God asked him, "Who told you that you were naked? Have you eaten of the tree of which I commanded you not to eat?" (Gen. 3:11). To which Adam replies with blame, "The woman you put here with me thought it would be a good idea to eat the fruit" (Gen. 3:12, author's wording). The woman, in turn, blames the snake (Gen. 3:13). Blame, as it were, is a defensive response. Blame is rooted in fear. When the world is seen through the lenses of winners and losers, zero-sum, blame is the most natural and obvious response. Of course, we don't usually call it blame when we are the ones blaming others. We call it a proper self-defense, or whatever. The bottom line is that we refuse to accept responsibility as that would require us to admit our sinful choices. Such an admission would leave us vulnerable, which we are trying to avoid. These are the effects of sin. Sin distorts our perspective of reality and our sense of responsibility. God brings the light of truth to bear on us in judgment, and it leads us to life, not death.

God proceeds to detail the consequences of Adam and Eve's sin. For the man, his work will unfold in an adverse and uncooperative context. He will be haunted by the sense of futility while joy will be fleeting in his best efforts. For the woman, the pain of bringing children into this world is as physical as it is emotional. It has as much to do with delivery as it does guiding and teaching children into young adulthood. Through it all, God promises to destroy the Adversary by the seed of the woman (Gen. 3:15). Jesus is the seed of the woman who will, despite the pain and suffering of bringing him into this world, claim victory over Satan on the cross. This victory assures the man and woman that God will not allow their pain and suffering to destroy them. God will use their struggle to shape them into people who glorify Him. Their call to work and be fruitful is vandalized by their sin. The effects of sin will linger even after Jesus conquers the Adversary on the cross. But, what Jesus starts at Calvary will be finished at His second coming. God's judgment brings salvation, not death.

He covers their nakedness with the skins of animals. He removes the covering they made and replaces it with His covering. Instead of giving them completely over to themselves, he comes looking,

The Isolation

and finds them. This is what God does from Genesis 3 all the way to the Cross on Calvary. He comes looking for the lost children, the sons and daughters of Adam and Eve.

God finds all of us afraid and busy trying to cover up our insecurity and indifference. He finds us angry and yet full of disappointment and hurt. Not only does God come looking, but He will not stop until we are located. God has gone to great lengths to find us in Jesus.

Some have been hurt by childhood abuse that has not only left deep pain, but stained all their relationships ever since. Some have committed crimes for which they feel ashamed and embarrassed, as though they are beyond the reach of God's grace. Others have been betrayed by a loved one and dedicated to living at a safe distance from others for the rest of their days. We are all cheaters, afraid, lonely, angry, and fighting for survival when the voice of God in Jesus reaches our hearts: "Come to me, all who labor and are heavy laden, and I will give you rest. Take my yoke upon you, and learn from me, for I am gentle and lowly in heart, and you will find rest for your souls. For my yoke is easy, and my burden is light" (Matt. 11:28–30).

Chapter 5:
The Community

We lay down the burden of hiding and pretending, which normally takes up such a dreadful amount of human energy. We engage and are engaged by others in the most profound depths of the soul.

—Dallas Willard, *Renovation of the Heart*

I was fresh out of graduate school with my degree in biblical counseling. The coursework and the community in which I studied brought a renewed sense of appreciation and urgency to forge meaningful friendships. As I searched for a place to work after graduation, my wife and I, along with our newborn son, were grateful when a call came from a community that included many dear friends. Accepting the position would bring us back into connection with people who had been formative in our early years of marriage. Now, as we started our family, these relationships were an especially precious gift from God. We were the youngest of all the couples. These friends were older than us, and being in their company brought much needed perspective and encouragement.

As I was settling into my role at the church where I worked, I

Go Outside

was looking for companionship. From that group of friends, four of us husbands began meeting early on Wednesday morning at a neighborhood Starbucks. Nearly every single Wednesday morning for several years, I met these men for coffee before we went our separate ways for the day. As consistent as we were in meeting, one of the men would call every Tuesday night to confirm we were still meeting! For all of us, this time proved invaluable as each one of us faced different challenges during that time in our lives. To this day, we are all still good friends. We no longer all live in the same town, but we look for every chance to meet and enjoy the gift of God in good friendship.

Do you have any friends?

Friendship takes time and honesty. To go beyond being mere acquaintances, people have to be deliberate about carving out time with one another. This effort and time is hard to justify in our busy lives. As basic a necessity as friendship is, it gets treated like a luxury in our fast-paced society. Yet, even in the paradise that was Eden in Genesis 1 and 2, "It was not good that man should be alone." If it was important in paradise, it is probably even more so in our day and age!

You might be thinking, but Chad, you don't know the way that people have let me down. That's true, I don't. But I've had my fair share of heartbreak and betrayal, too. My friendship with these men that I just spoke of was growing at a time when I was seeing a very ugly and divisive side of a church. I was young and not prepared for a situation that slowly emerged, grew steadily, and eventually divided staff members into factions that were pitted against one another. Looking back, I see where my younger self didn't always handle the struggle well. Yet, I also recall a lot of disappointment and disillusionment. This was a place where I had learned and grown as a leader and pastor. Within a matter of months, I was caught up in a situation that called into question every relationship

The Community

I had with staff. I was devastated and felt lost.

The situation had come to a head while we were at a fall staff retreat. We were there to rest and plan, trying to find some space to enjoy each other's company. It had been a busy season for the staff. Instead of forging ahead business-as-usual, I asked the senior pastor if we could take time to share hurts, disappointments, and areas in which we were struggling. What came next was more than I ever imagined. It was certainly more than the senior pastor knew about. But, as painful as it was to hear, it needed to be heard. In short, staff members were working long hours, felt very insecure about their work, didn't feel connected with others, and were starving for spiritual nourishment. Instead of this honest and open conversation leading to deeper and more honest relationships among the staff, the Enemy used it to "kill, steal, and destroy." It was the beginning of a season of fear, paranoia, gossip, divisiveness, and infighting. The following spring, I left. I had nowhere to go, but I knew I couldn't stay. It was too painful. Had I not left, I probably would have been fired. Over time, I had come to be seen as divisive and manipulative. Nothing I did could change this perspective. This was a time when I needed those friends at breakfast more than I could have ever imagined. They were true companions.

Far from a luxury, friendship is something we all need. We all need people who are nearby and not merely populating a list of "friends" on Facebook or followers on Instagram. We need people who do more than click through the pictures of our lives like spectators; we need people who are part of our lives and are helping to tell the story of our lives. We all need companions.

Eugene Peterson, the pastor and scholar who paraphrased the Bible into what is called *The Message*, was addressing a room full of pastors many years ago at a National Pastors' Conference in Southern California. One of the main points in his talk had to do with the importance of companionship in the pastor's life. He was going after the all too common reality in which pastors are competitors with other pastors and even their own congregation members. Peterson told the pastors that they needed people they could sit and break bread with. In fact, he explained, the root words *companion* came from Latin words that meant together (com) and bread (pan). His admonishment and insight was exactly what a roomful of spiritual leaders needed to hear. Not even pastors are exempt from being alienated. In fact, I might argue, pastors and ministry leaders are especially prone to soul-killing alienation.

When life is boiled down to "getting things done" and hyperproductivity, friendships and family can seem like obstacles threatening to impede our progress. This is what we saw in the last chapter as others become objects to be avoided or used in our effort to maximize our satisfaction in life. We are in such a hurry that friendship seems like a waste of time. This is deeply entrenched in our culture and our sinful hearts. In fact, "the power of sin," writes Frederick Buechner, "is centrifugal." This power pushes others toward the periphery of our lives.[7] *Do you have anyone with whom you are able to connect with in meaningful ways on a regular basis?*

Chances are you have probably been through difficult periods in your life when the value of friendships and family was clearly seen and felt. I met a man from Rwanda several years ago. He told stories of being a young boy on the run from warlords and genocidal violence. He said that he and his friends worked very hard to stick together while on the run, looking for safe cover. He had a saying that he and his friends would often recall, "You can run faster alone; but you can go farther together." If speed and short-term progress are all you care about, then life turns out to be very lonely. If a sustainable and livable rhythm is what you desire (it is

The Community

what you are made for!), then you need to travel through life with friends.

Community Restored

Recall the passage we have looked at from Romans 12:1–2. Having gained a view of God's mercies in and through Jesus, Paul calls the church to offer their "bodies as living sacrifices." This act of self-giving reflects the life of Jesus (Phil. 2:1–11) and it is the shape of one being freed from the power of sin. Living into this freedom means we are living in and enjoying relationships. We are participating in the life-giving sort of relationships for which we were made and which reflect the image of God: Father, Son, and Spirit. Christ-centered friendship, then, is a source of great joy because it is glorifying to God, our Maker.

Jesus went to great lengths to stress the fact that he would not leave his friends as orphans (John 14:18). Jesus sent his disciples to "all the nations" to build relationships for the purpose of making disciples. Toward the end of the Great Commission there is an important and often overlooked truth: "I am with you always, to the end of the age" (Matt. 28:20). Our connection with God through Jesus leads us *into* relationships and *supports* those relationships. As we see in Acts 2, the work of the Holy Spirit in and through the apostles resulted in gospel communities and the local church.

Acts is a book about the life and work of the apostles as God used them to plant the church: "Acts of the Apostles." A good friend of mine, however, likes to call it the Acts of the Holy Spirit! After all, he rightly reasons, while God used the lives of the apostles, it was the actions of the Holy Spirit that brought people from an array of backgrounds and spiritual contexts into the Body of Christ. That was true in the first century; it is still true today.

Go Outside

The planting of the church begins in Acts 2. Whereas God had scattered the people at the Tower of Babel in Genesis 11 by giving them different languages, God brings groups and tribes of people together through the work of the Holy Spirit at Pentecost. The apostles were given the ability to speak in languages they had not previously known so as to forge a community through the hearing of the Good News of Jesus.

The story in Acts 2 is dramatic and supernatural. It is the work of the Holy Spirit through ordinary men like Peter, James, and John. In recounting this story, Luke gives us a glimpse into these early communities. Having heard and responded to God's grace in the gospel, the people come together. They are "devoted" to the "apostles' teaching," "fellowship," "breaking bread," and praying together (Acts 2:42). They were continually in awe of what God was doing in their community and they were compelled to share what they had in order that they had nothing lacking (Acts 2:43–45).

From these early stages in the development of the local church, we learn that the gospel doesn't send us on a solitary spiritual pilgrimage. Scripture isn't asking us to join the church. The Good News of the Gospel is that we *are* joined to the Body of Christ. Now, even as you read this, the love of Jesus in its members directs their life together and their engagement with the larger community surrounding the local church. God's grace is made manifest to us through the community we share. This happens with other disciples who are growing in their knowledge and application of God's Word and who are on a Gospel Mission.

Once Paul had finished writing to the Roman church about the saving work of God in chapters 1–11, the apostle turns his attention to the practical outworking of God's grace among God's people. He begins with a call to be "living sacrifices" who do not think of themselves "more highly than" they ought. "For as in one

The Community

body we have many members, and the members do not all have the same function, so we, though many, are one body in Christ, individually members one of another" (Rom. 12:3–5). This one sentence gives us great insight into God's design for our lives. It is as simple as it is profound: In and of ourselves, we are incomplete. We are parts or members, but not the whole in and of ourselves. It is absurd, therefore, as one member of the body, to think the world revolves around us or to think we can manage on our own! It may be trite, but it is no less true, we need each other. Knowing that God has given me certain gifts should move me to be in community with others so that I can do what God has designed me to do and be the person God created me to be.

Think about that!

Reread that.

Reread Romans 12:3–5.

The gospel, then, *liberates* us to live for the glory of God in with God's family! Instead of using people for our benefit, we are seeking to serve one another and encourage one another in the faith. It is essential for Christ's followers, therefore, to gather with other believers, to share honestly, and support the work of God in one another.

I say it *liberates* us as a direct challenge to the notion of freedom and self-expression so ingrained in our modern culture. The idea of freedom in our modern culture means cutting ties with all constraints, obligations, and expectations so that you can really get to know and be yourself. This is the "wide gate" that Jesus described, which leads to destruction. The Way of Jesus is narrow and difficult, but it leads to life (Matt. 7:13–14). When it comes to knowing ourselves, and appreciating what we have to offer, this is not something we can do in isolation. While all of us have been

Go Outside

hurt and felt disappointment in relationships, it is in relationship with others that we learn and grow. The gospel breaks the power of hurt and mistrust and gives us grace to connect with people as God intended. Those connections are the soil out of which our gifts and talents flourish. Throughout Scripture and the story of God's redemptive plan for all of creation, He singles out individuals but always works in and through them within a larger context of community. The relationship between Abraham and Sarah plays a critical role in paving the way for Jesus.

God promised to Abraham (Gen. 12:2) to make his offspring a "great nation." This ordinary couple, with all of its shortcomings, would be the means through whom God would bring Jesus to save the world from sin. He first led this couple to leave their homeland; to be set apart for God's redemptive purpose. Not able to have children on their own, this couple figured God had it wrong or needed an alternative plan (Gen. 16).

Together, Abraham and Sarah had to trust that God would work in their weaknesses to fulfill His promise. This trust provided outbursts of laughter (Gen. 17:17)! Sarah did, however, get pregnant and gave birth to a little boy whose name means laughter, Isaac. From Isaac, we trace the lineage of David. These descendants pave the way for the birth of Jesus. Born to Mary and Joseph by a miracle of God, Jesus not only is the fulfillment of the promise made to Abraham and Sarah. But, his life, death, and resurrection prove that he is greater than all of the patriarchs in Israel's history. Romans 4 tells us that the true offspring of Abraham are those who are recipients of God's grace through Christ Jesus and thus our identification with the family depends upon faith (Rom. 4:16). As followers of Jesus, we are members of God's family! We are one of many countless stars in that nighttime sky in Genesis 15:5 or one grain of sand along the seashore in Genesis 22:17.

The Community

As we grow into this new identity with other family members, we are told to "put to death what is earthly" and to "put on...compassionate hearts" (Col. 3:5, 3:12). The disciples of Christ are called to "bear one another's burdens, and so fulfill the law of Christ" (Gal. 6:2). We cannot hope to grow without each other. There is within each member of Christ's Body a growing mindfulness of other people's interests and needs. In this way, we reflect Jesus and the law of love. This is just what Jesus did before dying on the cross. Jesus demonstrated his love for his disciples when he washed their feet. This is also the living demonstration for how the church is to love one another (John 13:34).

In addition to the community renewal within the broader family of God, the relationships between husbands and wives and their children is transformed by God's grace. For Paul, families become bright lights for the gospel of Jesus Christ. The way husbands love their wives and wives their husbands; the way children honor their parents and the way parents care for and instruct their children—these Christ-centered, God-fearing homes are an integral part of what God is doing in and through the church (Eph. 5; Col. 3:18–25).

Yet, in every town and county across our country, there are courtrooms dedicated to the dissolution, divorce, and breakup of the family. It's no wonder churches struggle with sin that tears at their communities since the families gathered in the church are being torn apart. This is a fact that early in my work as a church leader and pastor I was shocked to learn. Namely, those who were given charge to lead were going home every night to dying marriages, disbelieving children, and isolation in their own homes. This was a cruel fact that I learned during that difficult season I described above. Several of the leaders in that church arrived at their church office every morning with heavy and broken hearts. This glimpse gave me a deep passion and sense of purpose around helping those who lead to realize growing and vital lives in the community—both in their homes and in their churches.

In the 20 plus years we lived in Houston, I had the privilege of helping plant several different churches. I've also enjoyed and struggled as a pastor in the church. At the end of a long day of leading and talking and counseling, I'd get into my car and start making my way back home. When my children were younger, and Meeka stayed home with them, about halfway home I'd come out of the fog of my day's work and realize that I was about to walk into lots of activity, needs, noise, and demands on my time and energy. I'll be honest, I didn't always respond well in this transition. Sometimes I was grumpy and wanted to be left alone. *Not good!* At other times, I strapped on my Super Dad cape and set out to solve all the problems under our roof. This usually lasted about five minutes and then crumbled under my own frustration. It was after much failure and not handling this transition well that God got my attention one day. I didn't need a *cape*. I needed an *apron*. Instead of trying to be Superman, I needed to be a servant to my wife and my children. I needed to love them *as Jesus had loved me*.

This sort of mindset is simply not possible without the grace of God in Christ. I'm incapable of this on my own. Without Jesus, I'm stuck doing more and trying harder and getting even more frustrated. It's when I confess my limitations and rely upon Jesus that I'm able to love my family as God designed. My family doesn't need me to be a hero as much as they need me to be a humble servant of God's plans and purposes. A really great version of myself is a lousy version of Jesus! It is when I'm *dependent* upon God's grace as a father and husband that I'm *dependable* for my family. This, I'm utterly convinced, is one of the most compelling pictures of the gospel among our friends and other family members.

The Community

The local church and our own families are powerful pictures of God's design for companionship and community. But our friendships are too. Our friendships at work or in our free time can also draw our attention to God's glorious design for community—like the one I started this chapter telling you about.

Again, the gospel doesn't call us into a monastic life where we are walled off from the world in which we live. Romans 12 describes people who are striving to be a blessing to others in the community: "If possible, so far as it depends on you, live peaceably with all" (Rom. 12:18). Then, the writer of Hebrews instructs Jesus's followers, "Strive for peace with everyone, and for the holiness without which no one will see the Lord" (Heb. 12:14).

Do you have any friends? Sure, you may not be an outgoing extrovert. I'm not. Whatever your personality and disposition, are you involved in giving and receiving the blessing of others? You may have history that tells you people can't be trusted. But, the gospel assures Jesus's followers that the power of sin in betrayal and dishonesty will not have the final word. Armed with God's grace, we can know that nothing will separate us from God's love as we walk into a dangerous world by faith (See Romans 8).

In short, to build community is to embrace hope.

Few places in our world offer a more powerful glimpse of the gospel of Jesus Christ than a person or people whose love is self-sacrificial and whose involvement with others isn't self-centered. Conversely, few places cause more despair and cynicism than the hurt people inflict upon others. Paul says that among the three Christian virtues of faith, hope, and love, love is the greatest.

Why is love the greatest?

It is the greatest precisely because God is love, and, ultimately, it is

Go Outside

God's victory through Jesus that saves the world from the absence of love.

Chapter 6:
The Consumer

To be healed we must come with all the other creatures to the feast of Creation.

—Wendell Berry, *The Art of Commonplace*

In each of the previous sections, we have explored two key features of our humanity. Made in the image of God and made for the glory of God, we are created to enjoy a relationship with God (worship) and to enjoy relationships with each other. In this final section, we will explore a third aspect of our humanity shaped in the likeness of God: *stewardship*.

Stewardship is a practical and everyday part of our lives, often overlooked in our faith development. It entails the management and allocation of our time, talents, and treasures. It is the work that we do, the hobbies we enjoy, the exercise we do to stay fit, the skills we acquire, the money we earn, and the things we make. In short, we are created to manage all the gifts that God has given to us. Seeing ourselves as caretakers and seeing this as an essential part of our design influences many different aspects of our lives. As a mindset, *stewardship is seeing every resource in our possession as a gift from God to be used for God's pleasure and purposes.* As a way of life, *stewardship is living outside of a prison of consumption and in the wide-open space of growing, cultivating, crafting, and creating.* Just as sin has perverted our worship of God and our relationships with one another, so it has distorted how we care for the time, talent, and treasures of our lives.

Whereas worship has been turned into idolatry and people have been turned into objects for selfish ends, stewardship has been swallowed up by a belief system of consumerism: working for the immediate gratification at the lowest possible price. This fallen logic of sin turns us away from God, leading us to see ourselves as the sole generators of all that we want or need. Furthermore, that same fallen logic turns our hearts selfish. Not thinking of others, we hoard and protect what we wrongfully think belongs to us. In the end, we become slaves to our appetites and never find the satisfaction that we so desperately long for.

The focus of this chapter is understanding this logic and how it distorts our call to be stewards of God's gifts. I will first examine Genesis 1–3, which provides us a glimpse into how it is supposed to be and how things have gone so wrong. Then, in the next chapter we will look to Jesus for reconciling us to be the gardeners that God made us to be.

At Work in Paradise

Several years ago, my wife and I were given a gift. It was a room in an all-inclusive resort on a beach near Tulum, Mexico, just south of Cancun. It was a gift to us after a very busy season of work and parenting our three kids. And it was amazing! Here's what our days looked like in paradise:

Wake up midmorning. Enjoy a breakfast served to us in the

The Consumer

resort. Walk down to the beach and find the perfect spot to spend the day looking out at coral-blue water and enjoying the warmth of the Caribbean sun; swim and snorkel; welcome the waiter to bring us food and drink; walk back to our room, shower, and find a restaurant in the resort where we would eat dinner; return to the beach and enjoy the evening breeze and sound of the ocean; and fall asleep as we looked forward to doing it all over again the next day! This went on for nearly a week!

By the time we had to pack our bags and head home, I was, much to my surprise, ready to get back to our kids and into our normal routine. Don't get me wrong, it was amazing! But we couldn't have handled too many more days of all that relaxation! Something in me wanted to do more than just lie around while I stuffed my every desire with more and more. Something in me wanted to work, to get back to managing our lives—all that was part of a desire for stewardship.

In Genesis 1 and 2, God created a perfect place called Eden. God placed the man and woman in the garden and gave them work to do and commanded them to rest once every seven days. Have you ever stopped to think that they were working in paradise before sin entered the picture? That's because the entire story in Genesis 1 and 2 opens with *God at work*! The God who creates stamps man and woman with the desire for meaningful and fruitful work. Creating, managing, caring for, and cultivating are all reflections of God's image in the man and woman.

"In the beginning, God created the heavens and the earth. The earth was without form and void, and darkness was over the face of the deep. And the Spirit of God was hovering over the face of the waters" (Gen. 1:1–2).

The word "created" literally means to give form to or to shape something. Whatever was happening among the members of the

Go Outside

Holy Trinity in the great expanse of eternity before this moment, we don't exactly know. But what we do know in part is that God is working. God is shaping, forming, and fashioning heaven and earth. God is taking chaos and emptiness and bringing about order and structure. The Spirit of God is close at hand and involved in the nitty-gritty. Instead of throwing up His arms in frustration, God speaks into the chaos. It's hands-on, down-and-dirty, up-close work. Far from a distant cosmic being removed from creation, God is engaged with what is coming into being. Instead of silence in the face of what appears to be chaotic, *God speaks.*

"And God said…" is the opening line of the next scene (Gen. 1:3). God's voice penetrates the chaos in order to call into existence things that did not otherwise exist. John's Gospel in the New Testament tells us that this creative and powerful Word is Jesus, the second member of the Trinity! From the beginning of time, Jesus, the Word of God, has been calling into order that which is otherwise is disorderly. John says that "through him, and without him was not any thing made that was made" (John 1:3).

Not only is God at work, but the results are good. This fact is repeated throughout the creation narrative. Like an artist surveying his masterpiece, God surveys the work and sees that it is very good. The Hebrew word translated into saw or seeing (*raah*) implies more than just observation from a distance or observation in a clinical sense. God's survey of creation includes total and complete understanding of what has been made. The *seeing* God and the *speaking* God is the *working* God who is creating good things from chaos and disorder.

After the heavens and earth are made, Genesis 1:26 tells us that, "God said, 'Let us make man in our image, after our likeness.'" Instead of holding creation for the sole enjoyment of Father, Son, and Spirit, the Trinity creates man and woman and gives them

The Consumer

the mandate to care for and enjoy the creation. This act of creating is different than all that had gone before it. Male and female are God's appointed caretakers over the garden. Furthermore, they are created in the image of their Creator. Their being is rooted in who God is and what God does. Their position as caretakers is unique and without parallel in all of creation. "And let them have dominion over the fish of the sea and over the birds of the heavens and over the livestock and over all the earth and every creeping thing that creeps on the earth... Be fruitful and multiply and fill the earth and subdue it" (Gen. 1:26b, 28).

There it is! They are given a job to do in paradise! God gives them a gift: the earth and all that fills the earth. The words "dominion" and "subdue" go with the mandate to be fruitful, to enjoy, and to cultivate the garden. The life God breathes into the man and woman fosters the life of ground, sea, and forests. The man and woman are God's stewards and represent God's glorious purposes in creation.

Far from being a part of the curse, our desire to do meaningful work is a reflection of God in our humanity. But hard and meaningful work requires rest, too. Together, work and rest give our lives a rhythm for living and thriving in God's economy. Think about how different this biblical fact is in comparison to our Western consumeristic culture. So often we swing wildly between working like crazy and then collapsing in exhaustion, only to return to our unsustainable pace after a week's vacation. Our best efforts can hardly keep up with our voracious appetites and leveraged lifestyles. There's no letting up lest we miss a payment or miss an advancement at work. Rest is something we believe we'll do at our next vacation or when we retire from work altogether. But, this is not the cadence for which God has created us. The unsustainable pace and chaotic pattern in our working life can be traced all the way back to Genesis 3 and the fall of humanity from their God-glorifying position. In a sense, our work becomes an attempt to avoid or hide from God and each other.

Working to Hide

While God and humanity are intended to work together in caring for and cultivating creation, the moment the first man and woman disobey God in Genesis 3, their partnership is severely compromised. They fall from the place of balance God had intended for them. Immediately, the man and woman begin *working to cover nakedness and to hide themselves from God* (Gen. 3:8). Instead of hearing the sound of God's footsteps in the garden and looking forward to the work they would do with each other and with God, they experience fear and dread.

As we saw earlier, first and foremost, turning away from God means turning inward; this inwardness brings on an overdeveloped sense self-consciousness in Adam and Eve, and all their sons and daughters ever since. Feeling shame and contempt for this new perspective of their nakedness, the two get to work in a very different way and for different reasons than before. Instead of working for the glory of God and the good of each other, the first couple began working to compensate for their shame and insecurity: "They sewed fig leaves together and made themselves loincloths" (Gen. 3:7). But God came looking for them. Sensing God's movement in the garden sends the man and woman scrambling for more cover. Despite their best efforts to hide from God, thankfully and graciously, God found them.

"Who told you that you were naked?" God asked the man (Gen. 3:11). Adam stammered and stumbled and blamed Eve, and even God for that matter! No sooner had Adam done so, then God explained the consequences of their sin. God first warned the ser-

The Consumer

pent that its days were numbered and that the woman's offspring would utterly and totally defeat it (i.e., Jesus of Nazareth). God's attention, then, turned to the man and woman.

The greatest and most exquisite of human work, childbirth, which God gave to the woman in a special way, would come with much pain and suffering (Gen. 3:16). And to the man, God warned that "in pain you shall eat of [the ground] all the days of your life." If the woman's pain would be centered around the work of *procreating*, the man's pain would be in *providing*. In fact, God goes on to describe the gnawing sense of futility that would haunt everyman's work, "thorns and thistles it shall bring forth for you...By the sweat of your face you shall eat bread, till you return to the ground" (Gen. 3:18–19).

Again, work is not the result of the curse. But now, because of sin, our efforts are plagued with the question of purpose and effectiveness. Because of man's rebellion against God, the man will struggle under the weight of feeling like his work is useless. On the very best day without God, our work will function as a way to buy things so that we can escape our sense of futility. Or, work will altogether replace our need for God (or so we think) as we sacrifice everything and everyone to be successful in our work. The saying, "There's no rest for the weary," is an apt description of fighting and clawing for survival in our work apart from God. For some people, the work they do for gainful employment is toil and trouble; the work itself is demeaning, dangerous, or detrimental to their health. They are working to survive and looking forward to the next day off to escape from their struggle. For others, their work is highly regarded and they are well-compensated for the work they do. Their efforts result in vacations, big houses, lots of toys, and other distractions that lead them to believe that they don't need God outside of their own efforts. To illustrate this existential and economic dilemma,

Go Outside

the writer of Proverbs cries out to God:

> *Give me neither poverty nor riches;*
> *feed me with the food that is needful for me, lest I be full and*
> *deny you*
> *and say, "Who is the Lord?"*
> *or lest I be poor and steal*
> *and profane the name of my God.*
>
> Prov. 30:8–9

That is the voice of wisdom that comes from the fear of God. When we turn away from God and reject the wisdom of God, we become foolish. We struggle aimlessly in our work or we become absurdly addicted to our work, pretending to be like God. Beyond the places of our employment, the management of our lives becomes a struggle for satisfaction, and one long effort to avoid boredom. Instead of seeing God's hand as the source of all good gifts in our lives, we see ourselves as our sole provider. Instead of being caretakers, we become consumers. Instead of being able to really enjoy the bounty of God's presence in our lives, we are haunted by a feeling that the work we do is never enough. This becomes the launching pad that sends us from paycheck to paycheck, activity to activity, purchase to purchase, and so on.

Again, this sinful predicament with regards to our working life overlaps with and is connected to our worshipping life and community life. In Genesis 3, the first and most significant departure the man and woman made was from God's command. The couple listened to the serpent whose voice aroused their appetites for which the tree seemed the panacea. In this, they replaced God with their appetites. They turned away from God and began considering their desires apart from God's plans and purposes. The question and possibility of more, something better than the vocation given by God and satisfaction in God awakened in them. No

The Consumer

sooner had they turned from God than they were divorced from one another. Once they had turned loose of the security found in God's call upon their life, they were aimless except for the overwhelming need to hide, to take care of themselves. *So much of our modern-day consumerism is driven by this self-preoccupation to get as much as we can for ourselves.*

This relentless drive is more than a time management issue. It is more than a money management issue as well. If we start with those as the primary needs, we won't get to the root of our dissatisfaction. The only way out of this prison of consumption is to return to the Voice of the One through whom we were created. We must return to Jesus. In fact, Jesus extends us an invitation in Matthew's Gospel: "Come to me, all who labor and are heavy laden, and I will give you rest. Take my yoke upon you, and learn from me, for I am gentle and lowly in heart, and you will find rest for your souls. For my yoke is easy, and my burden is light" (Matt. 11:28–30).

Jesus is offering to save us from ourselves. He is offering to do for us a work we could never do. He is offering us rest for our souls. But, it's hard to hear Jesus amongst the noise of our busy lives; it's hard to see the gift that Jesus is extending to us amidst all the other promises of this world. I imagine that on the day Jesus made this invitation, there were some who couldn't wait to respond. I imagine them being pitiful and beat down. Others heard Jesus with their ears, but the success and striving in their heart kept them from responding. They couldn't really *hear* the invitation in their *heart*. They couldn't yet admit that they needed saving from their sinful selves.

God's grace in Jesus offers us rest for our soul and rhythm in our lives. In Jesus, the call to be stewards of God's creation and the gifts of God is restored and we are empowered by the Holy Spirit to do the job that God created us for in the beginning.

Chapter 7:
The Gardener

> Your obligation is to reach as deeply as you can and offer your unique and authentic gifts as bravely and beautifully as you're able.
>
> —Bill Plotkin, *Nature and the Human Soul*

Sin enters the story in Genesis 3, and makes the world small and complicated.

It has been doing that ever since.

Thinking that we'd be better off on our own and unshackled by God's purposes and design, we find the opposite is true. Increasingly focused on ourselves, we become more and more committed to getting what we want. But this self-expression doesn't lead us into wide-open spaces for which we were made; instead, we become protective and suspicious of everyone else. Like Adam and Eve feeling shame about their nakedness and hiding from each other and God, we become driven by fear and self-contempt. Instead of cultivating the gifts God has given to us, we become spiritual, emotional, and material hoarders.

Go Outside

It is in the midst of this mindset that God comes looking for Adam and Eve. "Where are you?" (Gen. 3:9). That search culminated in the person and work of Jesus who calls out to those burdened and beat down in hiding: "Come to me…and I will give you rest for your soul" (Matt. 11:28). Hearing God's voice through faith unlocks the prison of sin and leads us into the adventure for which we were made. We come alive to the knowledge of God and to the fact that God knows us—even better than we know ourselves. What's more, God loves us and reestablishes us in the good life for which He made us. Even King David was desperate for God's gracious rescue, which he celebrates in Psalm 18: "He brought me out into a broad place; he rescued me, because he delighted in me" (Ps. 18:19).

This is where we have been thus far in the book. If at times these concepts have seemed overly spiritual or impractical, I appreciate your patience! What we are about to explore is how, in many ways, the redemptive work of God through Jesus has implications in how we spend our time, talents, and treasures. God made us to be stewards of these gifts, which are manifested in the practical, daily, and ordinary aspects of our lives.

Preparation

Over the years, I have had the privilege of taking many of our friends on backpacking trips. The better prepared we are for time on the trail, the better the trips go. There are always surprises in the wilderness and the unexpected will always be found, but good preparation enables you to respond to these instead of reacting and panicking.

This preparation includes getting your body ready to hike for several days at a higher altitude with weight on your back. Before you start thinking that this sounds like a torture fest, you should know that over the years, I've seen people of all shapes and sizes,

The Gardener

skills, and abilities enjoy themselves on the trail! Again, the key is good preparation. When it comes to your body, one of the greatest gifts God has given to you and me, hydration and aerobic exercise in preparation goes a long way once we are on the trail. The self-inflicted pain and suffering of exercise, in other words, will minimize the pain and suffering you might experience on the trail; it certainly minimizes unexpected injuries. When people fail to prepare their bodies, it's not very far into the hike when they meet up with regret.

Instead of turning around and heading back to where we started, the power and encouragement of community becomes increasingly important when the physical demands take their toll. There is something to be said about spending time alone in the wilderness; the solitude can be a powerful avenue through which God speaks to your heart. But, on our trips, we are traveling as a community. When you choose to take a hike with others, your individualistic plans are subject to the group. For starters, the group moves as fast as the slowest person. This can be the real test for both the strongest and the weakest hiker, but for very different reasons. It requires maturity on both ends to set aside personal pride and embrace the imperfect, less-than-ideal circumstances.

The emotional fitness of individuals enables them to defer to the needs of others on the trail. Long before the person takes to the backpacking trail, the depth and quality of their relationships prepare them to meet the daily challenges of living in community.

Preparation, then, begins with the exercise we subject our bodies to before the trailhead and the good habit of living in real community on a daily basis. This is true not only for backpacking, but in life. Being a steward of the gifts God has given us requires that we make preparations for the days ahead, the unexpected circumstances, and challenges we will inevitably face. These gifts are to be cultivated and nourished. If we fail to take care of our bodies and we neglect the need for community, we are not being faithful stewards. In doing so, we are setting ourselves up for knee-jerk reactions and anxious living in every facet of life. The pain of exercise and being slowed down in life, because of the demands of relationships, is worth the wisdom, insight, and patience that is cultivated in our hearts and minds. Patience, it has been said, counts for more than IQ in most settings when it comes to sustainable, long-term effort in whatever we do in life.

Good preparation enables us to respond instead of living reactionary lives. I have heard it said that being responsible is simply *being able to respond*. Being able to respond, then, requires cultivating the gifts God has given to us, whether it be our physical or emotional fitness.

Pursuing selfish, shortsighted ends in life may have quick payoffs but will be costly in the long run. Paul admonishes the church in Rome, which was suffering a great deal under the Roman emperor: "For by the grace given to me I say to everyone among you not to think of himself more highly than he ought to think, but to think with sober judgment, each according to the measure of faith that God has assigned" (Rom. 12:3). Being a good steward, then, begins with having a sober view of oneself and enjoying the wisdom of discipline and community.

This is what the Bible calls sanctification. Sanctification is the process by which we partner with the Holy Spirit at work in our lives to "work out our salvation with fear and trembling" into all the details of our time, talents, and treasures. Like apprentices of Jesus, it is where we learn to live into the rest that He has established in our souls. We are learning the art of living in the rhythms of God's grace. The fruit of working with the Holy Spirit includes love, joy, peace, patience, kindness, gentleness, goodness, faithfulness, and

The Gardener

self-control (Gal. 5:22–23).

Elsewhere in his letters, Paul compares the sanctifying preparation to that of a runner preparing for the big race. Instead of negating the grace of God, self-discipline is an act of faith in believing that God will use all of our efforts for His glory. "I discipline my body," he writes, "and make it my slave, so that, after I have preached to others, I myself will not be disqualified" (1 Cor. 9:27 NASB). Not only does taking charge of his body enable him to grow strong for his missionary journeys, it becomes a matter of integrity as he leads God's people through the preaching of the Word!

So, as Jesus's disciples, you and I are called to prepare for the journey ahead, which includes taking care of our bodies. In Western culture, especially in the United States, people can easily fall into the trap of worshipping their bodies. Instead of training your body to be your slave so that you can be God's servant, physical fitness and beauty become ends in themselves. The truth and grace of Scripture is used to keep us focused on the big picture of God's glory in our struggle against sin. At its root, sin turns the gifts of God into objects of worship. Again, in his letter to the Roman church, Paul warns against such deception: "For although they knew God, they did not honor him as God or give thanks to him, but they became futile in their thinking, and their foolish hearts were darkened" (Rom. 1:21). Good reparation begins by seeing our bodies and our relationships as gifts to be cared for and cultivated for God's purposes in our lives. *Sanctification is preparation for the journey to which we have been called.*

Packing Stations

The other part of preparing for several days on the backpacking trail is deciding what to bring. With a backpack strapped to your body and the limited space that it affords you, the decision process includes leaving many things behind! The professional guides at Noah's Ark Whitewater Rafting and Adventures in central Colorado call this moment of truth "packing stations." They get everyone in a circle with all their stuff they plan on bringing on the trail. Once each person's stuff is piled up in front of them, the guides begin handing out the community gear that must be taken and must be spread out amongst the group for the duration of our trip. The once modest piles of personal effects quickly grow into bulky loads. With limited space in a backpack and the truth about how much a backpack can weigh, people start making tough decisions. The task of getting their personal gear and their community gear into the small compartments forces everyone to simplify. Everyone has to ask themselves questions like: *Do I really need this? What are the necessities? What would I like to bring and what do I really need?*

All of us are tempted to complicate our lives with things that we are convinced we can't live without only to find ourselves weighed down with "creature comforts." I've seen the most seasoned and skilled outdoorsmen bring a bag full of gadgets that add very little value to their life on the trail, but instead adds weight to their packs and distracts them from the beauty of our surroundings. And I'm saying this as a person who loves the gadgets!

Life on the trail affords time to escape from the hustle and bustle of one's normal routine. It is time to turn away from distractions and focus on the beauty of God's unencumbered and wild creation. It is a time to get a better view of God and to see in creation how God loves and cares for us. All too often, the best intentions notwithstanding, our getaway gets away from us.

I'm talking about the difference between being a wise steward and a foolish consumer. Just as is the case with our bodies and our relationships, the amount of clutter in our lives can hamper us from being able to adequately respond; weighed down by stuff, we are

The Gardener

no longer nimble when life's challenges require us to be responsive. Instead of being resourceful and creative, we become panicked and stuck. In these moments, we realize that all the tools we thought would make our lives better have turned us into a tool! We lose our resourcefulness and skill to solve problems as we become overly dependent on useless gadgets. I find this happens a lot with technology that purports to help us manage our time and make plans. Very often, these become an end instead of a means!

Does this seem completely detached from your spiritual development as a disciple of Jesus? If so, that's because we have convinced ourselves that the world is divided into a secular/physical/nonspiritual realm and a sacred realm. The former is the area of tools and technology and the stuff of life; the latter is ephemeral and ethereal ideals. That is a lie!

When God created Adam and Eve, I think we can all agree that is a very spiritual as well as physical moment. He breathes life into Adam's body; He creates Eve out of Adam's flesh. God calls them to work! As we saw in the previous chapter, God designed and created them and then immediately employed them to be His caretakers. There's no distinction between what is physical and what is spiritual. Likewise, when the couple disobey God, the immediate effects entailed their whole being and their whole world. Eyes wide open, they began making things so they could hide from each other and God. This demonstrates that the spiritual reality is connected to the physical reality of our lives and vice versa. Sin manifests itself in our lives by making the world smaller and more complicated; it doesn't get divided up into physical (bad) and spiritual (good).

Realizing that God created us to be managers, creators, and overseers opens our eyes to see that every aspect of our lives is crying out to be cared for—this includes our stuff. The more stuff we mindlessly consume, the more out of control our lives become,

Go Outside

disabling our ability to respond to the world in which we live with love and generosity. We have fewer connections to people and the realities around us. We grow distracted in our stuff. Again, time on the trail with my belongings strapped to my back walking alongside of my friend, who is in the same situation, makes this point crystal clear. The heavier and more unnecessary my load is, the less connected I feel to my friend and the drudgery I experience on the journey.

For this reason, Jesus instructed his disciples to lighten their loads on their missionary journeys (Luke 9:3–6). Their physical load, which he warned should be light, was intricately connected to their spiritual calling as his missionaries. Their simplicity was reflected in every aspect of their lives. While we may not be called to travel throughout the world as a missionary, we are missionaries in the world *where we live*. What Jesus instructed his first disciples applies to his disciples today. We need wisdom that comes from God the Father in order to manage and moderate between the needs that we have and the wants that beg for satisfaction. We need to know that this discernment unfolds as much on an emotional level as it does on a rational level.

Unchecked, this consumer appetite, which is inspired by relentless and strategic marketing in our culture, can be our undoing. Once we are driven by our appetites instead of our Lord, we wind up in a prison of our own making. In this prison, work feels like slavery, instead of something for which we were created and called to. We get lost in our things and we lose sight of the main thing—glorifying God and enjoying God in all that we do and all that we have! Jesus comes looking for us and calls us out of these prisons to himself.

Go outside!

The Gardener

What You See Is What You Get!

Jesus told the people in Matthew 6 to look for God's strong and bountiful hand in the little things all around them: birds, flowers, and grass. Observe how God takes care of the birds. He then reassured them that if God cares for grasses and flowers like that, how much more so will he take care of them.

Open your eyes to see God's goodness and beauty and the blessing that He has provided. Open your eyes to see that God has invited you into the work of caring for and cultivating the resources He has created and given to you. Instead of feeling sorry for yourself, God calls you to get to work alongside of Him. Stop looking at what you don't have or how your life compares to your neighbor's and start looking at the riches of God throughout the world.

Annie Dillard is a writer whose nonfiction consists of books, letters, and essays that describe a vibrant, complex, and living world hidden right before our eyes. She writes about how when she was a little girl, her bedroom window overlooked a sidewalk in front of her house. With a view of people walking past her home, she enjoyed a peculiar activity as a way to engage and surprise the people passing by.

When no one was looking, she would hide pennies all the along the sidewalk in front of her home. She would stuff copper treasures into cracks and beneath trees along the way. Then, she would draw arrows indicating where the "gifts from the universe" could be found. Much to her surprise and dismay, the people rarely followed the arrows to the gifts she had hidden. Upon reflection, she writes, that's how most of us end up living our lives: what difference does a penny make? This, Dillard points out, is true poverty. It's a sort of despair and blindness. The world, she points out, is strewn in pennies! If you and I took the time to pick up all the loose change we found along the way, our pockets would be full of gifts from the universe. She concludes, "What you see is what you get."[8]

What do you see?

The gospel opens our eyes to see that salvation isn't merely a spiritual reality that secures our eternal state. The gospel transforms our whole life and how we see our time, talents, and treasures. These are gifts from God. He has placed us in a bountiful garden, which is full of weeds. While the work is hard and difficult for now, our "blessed hope" in Christ Jesus assures us that choosing to live simple, prepared, and purpose-filled lives matters. God the Father created us to be His partners in creation and has restored us to these positions in Christ. Together, we work for the glory of God and not just our own selfish ends.

The work we do in this world, with our hands or our minds, is a thanksgiving offering to God. What we do as God's stewards brings hope to the world and casts an alternative vision to that of mindless and selfish consumption. We need not be thrown off mission nor can we lose focus in the face of unexpected challenges that happen in our work. God promises to give us wisdom and insight so that we can respond with grace and truth.

We need not be locked away in a monastery to show that we love God; instead, we can point people to God in the good we do as we manage and use the talents God has given us. Having seen the blessings of God strewn throughout our lives like pennies hidden on the sidewalk, what we see is a future inaugurated with Christ's resurrection that promises to be even better than the one we enjoy now. Instead of being overcome with cynicism or despair, we are working toward a new heaven and a new earth. The work we are doing now is paving the way for that blessed day when all things will be made new.

In the final chapter, I will explore what it means to live in the now

The Gardener

and the not yet. I will explore the long and honored tradition of those who are waiting and watching for Jesus's return.

Chapter 8:
Headed Home

> To be a castaway is to search for news from across the seas.
> —Walker Percy, *Message in a Bottle*

Where are we? What is this place we call home?

At the time of writing this book, there are estimated to be over 60 million people around the world who are displaced and in search of a new home. Over 400,000 people have been killed in the civil war in Syria; of those, over 50,000 are children.

Closer to home, racism and bigotry continue to haunt this country. Groups that had all but been marginalized in our country are newly emboldened to spread their hatred and intimidation of others simply based upon their race, ethnicity, or religion. It's as sickening as it is divisive, and it tears at the fabric of our democracy. To make matters worse, our political leaders are polarized and unable to effectively lead the country.

If you turn to the local church, there are plenty of imperfections and blemishes to make one cringe. Just recently, I watched a video online in which another young pastor resigned from a large church because he was "leading on empty," an apparent reference to burnout and fatigue. I would later learn that the pastor had multiple affairs.

Simply put, this is not the way it's supposed to be.

Take the three areas of our humanity as designed by God that we have looked at in this book. In each of the three, we can easily see evidence of vandalism and distortion. With regards to worship, people have exchanged God's absolute glory for fleeting beauty; relationships are plagued by divorce and betrayal; and we've forfeited our roles as cultivators and become consumers. As King Solomon mourned in Ecclesiastes: "And whatever my eyes desired I did not keep from them. I kept my heart from no pleasure, for my heart found pleasure in all my toil, and this was my reward for all my toil. Then I considered all that my hands had done and the toil I had expended in doing it, and behold, all was vanity and a striving after wind, and there was nothing to be gained under the sun" (Eccles. 2:10–11).

Throughout this book, I've tried to describe worship, relationship, and stewardship as God's great gifts for human flourishing and, tragically, the areas where we see the greatest losses. As we come to the end, I neither pretend to have easy answers nor do I believe we have reason to despair. I've seen enough in my own short life to feel the pang of a groaning deep from within. The groan sometimes feels like anger or frustration or sorrow; but it always comes from a place of deep dissatisfaction and discontentment.

So, in this final chapter, I want to fully and honestly acknowledge that while we are meant to flourish in worship, relationship, and stewardship, we are living in a world where survival feels like the chief end of man. Instead of sons and daughters, pilgrims and strangers seems more like it. You and I may not be one of the 60 million immigrants displaced in this world, but we feel a growing sense of homesickness.

With this honest assessment, my hope is that honest confession leads to both a renewed hope in God's promises and a practical guide to finding beauty on our way.

Go Outside: Be Honest about the Struggle

First, if as followers of Jesus we commit to pretending the world is better than it actually is, we reveal a very shallow faith and an empty hope. One needs to go no further than the Scriptures to see the combination of a brutal honesty about the struggles people faced alongside of a deep and profound faith in God.

Given the struggles just outside of our door (not to mention our pews), the church can be tempted to retreat into the safety of its four walls. We do this by disengaging from our communities, by ignoring the struggles around us, and by crafting sermons, songs, and liturgies that lack honesty. Again, the Scriptures show us the way to both lament and celebrate, and cry out in anguish and in joy. Psalms is a great place to start: "I am feeble and crushed; I groan because of the tumult of my heart. O Lord, all my longing is before you; my sighing is not hidden from you" Ps. 38:8–9.

We forget that there's a book of Lamentations in our Bible! The prophet Jeremiah wrote these laments while serving the Lord. In the third chapter, the prophet cries out in pain, anger, and disillusionment. The following is a sample of the first third of this chapter:

> *He (God) has made my teeth grind on gravel,*
> *and made me cower in ashes;*
> *my soul is bereft of peace;*
> *I have forgotten what happiness is;*

Go Outside

> *so I say, "My endurance has perished;*
> *so has my hope from the Lord."*
>
> Lam. 3:16–18

Few people know that these verses are the immediate context for a hymn that is taken from this passage. I grew up singing this hymn in the church for years, before I realized the dark and difficult context from which it was taken:

> *But this I call to mind,*
> *and therefore I have hope:*
> *The steadfast love of the Lord never ceases;*
> *his mercies never come to an end;*
> *they are new every morning;*
> *great is your faithfulness.*
>
> Lam. 3:21–23

The great mercies of God are often lost on Christians who refuse to face the struggles in their own lives or in the world in which they live. As someone once said, the opposite of faith isn't doubt; it is indifference. For us to truly believe and to love God means that we will struggle with God in this world. Let us, as the sons and daughters of God sing our songs with full-throated honesty as we stand on the holy and victorious ground of Calvary.

The cynics of the world are most surprised by and unprepared for a church who leaves the four walls, engages the struggles of this world, and boldly lives out their love for God and others. While it may seem safer to retreat, it is not safety that Christ came to give to us. The adventure of knowing God and being known by God leads us outside of our safety zones and into the pain and suffering of the world.

Headed Home

Go Outside: Be Aware of the Beauty

If the church is guilty of retreating into the perceived safety of its four walls, it's also at a loss to know what to do with the beauty of this world. Hence, the subculture of Christianity often feels the need to create its own version of everything and make sure the world knows that it is Christian. Whether it's music, art, movies, theme parks, or neckties, the unfortunate result of these efforts can be second-rate and cheap substitutes. And, in a world that is hurting as badly as this one, we, of all people, ought to be leading the search for and finding the beauty of God all around us.

Concerning the beauty hidden in plain sight, I quoted Thomas Merton in the introduction of this book: "One of the most important—and most neglected—elements in the beginnings of the interior life is the ability to respond to reality, to see the value and the beauty in ordinary things, to come alive to the splendor that is all around us in the creatures of God. We do not see these things because we have withdrawn from them."[9]

Faith, hope, and love are the virtues of the Christian life. They take root in our heart by God's grace and flourish on our journey with the Holy Spirit throughout our lives. Knowing that we would see and experience troubling times in this life, Jesus assured us that God would provide for our needs and, through the Holy Spirit, would never leave us. Merton points to the ordinary and often overlooked blessings of our daily lives as the context for vital and strong interior lives. When we get into a hurry and are pushed and pulled by the frenetic pace of this world, we disconnect from the beauty of God and we starve the faith, hope, and love that is growing in us.

The more experience we have with the pain and disappointment of this world, the less like children we become; the more indifferent and bored we grow with the world in which we live. Enjoying the

Go Outside

little things seems childish and naive, at best. Yet, Jesus called us back to this childlike posture in Mark 10:15, as a means by which we enter into the kingdom: "Truly, I say to you, whoever does not receive the kingdom of God like a child shall not enter it." In his letter to the Romans, Paul described the cry of the faithful like that of a child.

The church in Rome at the time of Paul's letter was under heavy persecution. Paul reassured them that of all that they had to worry about in the world, God's love and care for them wasn't one of those things! Having been brought to life by the Spirit of God, they could freely cry out to God, "Daddy!" or "Pappa!" (Rom. 8:15). It's like we grow old and cynical in our faith when we no longer see and experience the beauty of this world, which leads us to see God's goodness and sovereignty. All we can see is the pain and suffering. Paul is calling Christians to a childlike faith in God. He's also acknowledging the groan of this existence. "For we know that the whole creation has been groaning together in the pains of childbirth until now. And not only the creation, but we ourselves, who have the first fruits of the Spirit, groan inwardly as we wait eagerly for adoption as sons, the redemption of our bodies" (Rom. 8:22–23).

Groaning inwardly and waiting expectantly is, in other words, part of what it means to be a child of God on this earth. A child wakes up every day to the very real possibility of delight and disappointment. And, so we, the children of God, can give ourselves over to the journey knowing that God the Father will guide us as we encounter both.

Go Outside: Be on the Lookout for More

Finding little nuggets of beauty along the way awakens desire. C.S. Lewis said that when we experience desires in this world that have no apparent satisfaction, we can rest assured knowing that we are made for another world.[10] And, so, I want to leave you, as it were, standing on the seashore waiting and longing for more. We are called to live in the present, while looking forward to the future, when our "blessed hope" will appear on the horizon and we will know that home is just up ahead!

The people in God's story who were faithful wanted more. These are the people who are mentioned in Hebrews 11. Starting with Abraham, the writer tells how Abraham set out from his home country and all his kinsmen and followed God to a promised land where he pitched his tents. His faithfulness, the writer points out, was an indication that Father Abraham "was looking forward to the city that has foundations, whose designer and builder is God" (Heb. 11:10). But, like Abraham and all the others in this roll call of faithfulness,

> *These all died in faith, not having received the things promised, but having seen them and greeted them from afar, and having acknowledged that they were strangers and exiles on the earth. For people who speak thus make it clear that they are seeking a homeland. If they had been thinking of that land from which they had gone out, they would have had opportunity to return. But as it is, they desire a better country, that is, a heavenly one.* Therefore God is not ashamed to be called their God, for he has prepared for them a city.
>
> Heb. 11:13–16, emphasis added

If God is not ashamed of my wandering and longing, then that means I can experience His love and presence in my searching. When my expectations are not met in this world, God is not telling me to lower my expectations. He is stoking the fires of desire in my gut. If I, like the people in Hebrews 11, continue hoping for more, I will experience God's pleasure and will not be disappointed. I can be both honest about how far short this world falls in my hopes and dreams. And, I can look forward with great expectations!

Writing in the first half of the last century, G.K. Chesterton described how he had been told, while growing up and in all his education, that modern culture marked a high watermark for humanity. Yet, he confesses, he struggled: "The modern philosopher had told me again and again that I was in the right place, and I had still felt depressed even in acquiescence. But I had heard that I was in the wrong place, and my soul sang for joy, like a bird in spring… [this explained why] I could feel so homesick at home."[11]

His heart "sang for joy" at the good news that this was the "wrong place"! In other words, he was told that he had arrived; he was living in the best, most modern, most advanced, and most beautiful places in human history. Yet, he was unsettled by the gnawing sense of being lost; he was homesick at home. It wasn't until his faith awoke him to the home for which he truly longed that joy and singing came!

When we are honest about our desire for more, our songs become richer, our prayers more faithful, and our love more like Jesus's love. With God's love at work in us and through us, we are far from passively waiting on the next best thing to happen.

No!

Instead, we become actively involved in promoting and telling others that there is something better, something more for which they long and that God promises to satisfy. Time and again, the gospels tell stories of Jesus doing this with the people he met. The story of the Samaritan Woman (John 4:1–26) is a powerful and beautiful example of how Jesus graciously pointed to her disappointment and failures while promising something more. There was plenty of water for her mouth in Jacob's well; but the cool drink of unconditional love had not been found in any of the beds she shared with her five partners. She was homesick and, like a lot of us, didn't even know it until she met Jesus. Jesus resurrected her desire for more!

Go Outside: To the Cheers of Those Who Have Gone before Us

The writer of Hebrews describes those who have gone before us and suffered because of their faith. They are a "great cloud of witnesses" encouraging us to stay the course. Concerning these faithful pilgrims, "the world was not worthy" of them (Heb. 11:38). The passage goes on to describe the most amazing and mind-blowing event. You and I will walk through the gates of the City of God with those who have gone before us. Instead of us entering into God's presence individually, we will enter as a community (Heb. 11:40) and receive our heart's satisfaction together. "Therefore," the writer says, "let us lay aside every weight, and sin which clings so closely, and let us run with endurance the race that is set before us, looking to Jesus, the founder and perfecter of our faith" (Heb. 12:1–2).

Our worship of God, our relationships with others, and our stewardship of the gifts we have been given are fixed points from which we can get readings concerning our location relative to God's plans and purpose for us. In this journey, when our homesickness can threaten our faith and hope and love, we can ask ourselves:

Where am I in relationship to God?

Where am I in relationship to others?

How am I managing my time, talent, and treasures?

Go Outside

With the gracious guidance of the Holy Spirit, we'll get a sense of our location and find the courage and faith needed to continue. We'll draw near to the God who is closer than we ever expected. We'll find companions on the way and thus avoid isolation on the journey. And, we'll find that God will provide for all of our needs; our cups will overflow! With God's help, we'll go outside! We'll "walk by faith" and know that on the appointed day, the City of God will greet us and we'll enjoy our homecoming!

Afterword: The Potter's Hands

All that man is capable of admiring is possible with God.
—Simone Weil, *Waiting for God*

Go outside.

After reading this book, it is my hope that you never hear that simple phrase the same way. God gives us a grand and gracious invitation in Christ Jesus. We are to leave behind the closed off, ever-shrinking, survivalist mentality that sin breeds. Instead, we are to enter into the space of faith, hope, and love! We've ended up in these small, cramped spaces by our own sinful choices and the sin of others in this world; our reactions and actions have led us deeper into the predicament, which is where Jesus finds us and rescues us. My humble quest has been to remind you of what Christ has done for you in restoring your heart for true worship, your longing for meaningful relationship, and urge to make something in this world with your time, talents, and treasures.

There are so many characters in Scripture who had to be reminded of who they were, their true story, and the shape of their lives.

Go Outside

Count Jeremiah among them! This prophet had the unfortunate task of preaching and prophesying on behalf of God to Israel, Jeremiah's own people. He was mocked, imprisoned, and shunned. One day, amidst his struggle to remain faithful to God, he was led by God to the potter's house. Once there, Scripture says that God "let him hear his words" (Jer. 18). The opening lines of this passage about the potter's house remind me of a similar experience I've had.

I once took a sculpting class in college in order to use some of my elective course hours. Much to my surprise and enjoyment, this was a dirty, sweaty sort of work. Being so hands-on and working so hard over a piece of artwork brought a whole new dimension to art and gave me a greater appreciation for sculptors and potters. As much as I enjoyed it, I was constantly reminded of my novice skills. While at times this was discouraging, there was much to enjoy all around me. I especially liked watching my classmates and professor, who were talented artists, start with formless blobs and piles of material and create something provoking, evocative, and beautiful. My eyes were drawn to their hands. It was as if their hands and fingers worked magic, translating into reality what their minds imagined. That image has stuck with me over the years. It inspires me to this day!

Many years after I took the class, I started an organization dedicated to providing spiritual direction and care, especially to those who lead local churches. *Spiritual formation is the gracious and powerful work of God done in us by the Holy Spirit of God that started with the work of Jesus on the Cross.* He is restoring our hearts to worship Him alone, to enjoy life-giving relationships, and to create things of real value in this world. That class has helped me as I have sought to facilitate and serve God's efforts in other people's lives. Being involved in a person's spiritual transformation is an honor

Afterword: The Potter's Hands

and it is humbling. I also have to be reminded that God is at work in my own life; it's easy to feel like I'm just spinning out of control on the wheel.

There are five truths we can take away from this peek into the potter's house.

First, and perhaps most obvious, this place is called the potter's house. The only thing not spinning in this house is the potter! He is fixed, purposeful, and active. All the creations reveal *the potter's* glory. It's all about the potter! Being in a relationship with God is like clay in the potter's hands—he looms ever larger, more powerful. As God looms larger, we see ourselves more truthfully.

Second, we are the clay. While we may appear potter-like in many of our roles in business, parenting, or studying, we are first and ultimately blobs of clay in the hands of the potter. This is what I call being right-sized. This is critical in the process. Recall the apostle Paul's response to being right-sized? A simple exclamation: "Oh!" (Rom. 11:33). Job has a similar response to God's expansive display: "Behold, I am of small account; what shall I answer you? I lay my hand on my mouth. I have spoken once, and I will not answer; twice, but I will proceed no further" (Job 40:4–5).

Third, we may be unsightly, unremarkable, and think we are spoiled beyond use. But, we are on the potter's wheel! There's no shame in the potter's hands. There's no arrogance, either. Neither shame nor pride bring about God's intended shape for our lives. Yielding to God's hand at work in our lives is a lot like a wrestling match. Again, Jacob knew this all too well! In this way, spiritual formation is the gracious and loving imposition of God. Sometimes it is being "made to lie down in green pastures," while at other times it is being led by "still waters" (Ps. 23:2).

Go Outside

Fourth, it is messy in the potter's house and it is not solitary confinement! Everywhere you look there is evidence of a potter at work and the fruit of his labor. There are all kinds of vessels in various stages of completion to be used for all kinds of purposes. Though we are blobs, the Spirit of God has quickened us to partner with what God is doing in us. Paul encourages us to "work out your own salvation with fear and trembling, for it is God who works in you, both to will and to work for his good pleasure" (Phil. 2:12–13). We *aren't* called to compare ourselves with each other. We are called, together, to partner with what God is doing in us and through us.

Finally, what is the potter doing? Simply put: whatever the potter wants! The form and shape of the vessel doesn't really come into view until the latter stages. Between the now and the not yet, we will join the chorus in all of creation as we "groan inwardly as we wait eagerly" (Rom. 8:23) for God's finished work and our full adoption! Along the way we are confident that God doesn't waste anything. My life is spinning, sometimes faster than I'd like. As long as God has His hands on me, I have hope! The one who calls you, who scooped you out of the mud, is faithful; he will shape you (1 Thess. 5:24, my paraphrase).

So, to review:

In the potter's house, it's all about the potter. To this point, the only thing not spinning is the potter's hands.

In the potter's house, we are the clay—blobs of clay in the potter's hands.

In the potter's house, our deformity is in the potter's hands.

In the potter's house, it is a messy place filled with the creation of the potter's hands,

Afterword: The Potter's Hands

In the potter's hands, nothing is wasted.

So much has been lost as a result of our sinful rebellion against God. Yet, in Christ, tattered and beaten by the struggles of this world, hope persists. Whatever condition we may find ourselves in, whatever stage in the process of becoming we may be, God is gracious and loving toward us. His unmerited favor is planted in our hearts by faith in Christ Jesus. There's no mistaking the origin of this gift! We are merely the vessels by which God has chosen to reveal Himself to the world. Broken and cracked though we may be, we are not defeated by our sin nor the sin of this world. We will persevere with this grace. This is Paul's admonishment to the Corinthians:

> *But we have this treasure in jars of clay, to show that the surpassing power belongs to God and not to us. We are afflicted in every way, but not crushed; perplexed, but not driven to despair; persecuted, but not forsaken; struck down, but not destroyed.*
>
> 2 Cor. 4:7–9

Acknowledgments

This book has the fingerprints of all the people who have been used by God to shape my life. I'd like to acknowledge a few of those gracious investors.

Over 27 years ago I met my wife. Meeka, you have been my constant companion and greatest encourager. Thank you for all of your love and patience; you know more than anyone else that this book is not the product of expertise but of God's grace at work in my life. Thanks for being part of that work for nearly three decades!

Reece, Noah, and Aimee…after your mom, you have been God's great invitation to keep going outside! I can't imagine my life without you. Each of you are unique reflections of God's glory in this world. I love you!

Mom and Dad, you sent me on my very first backpacking trip! Along the way, you have been undying in your love and faithfulness to me and to God's work in my life. Thank you!

Jeremy McQuown, you are a good and kind man. I couldn't think of a better person to be leading out at BetterDays! Thanks for your hard work and partnering in this vision of care and support to those who lead.

Go Outside

Harold and Diane McGowen, this project would not have been possible without your generosity and kindness. You have been faithful friends and generous with your encouragement in my life and in my family's life. Words cannot express how much I appreciate you and your family.

Susan and Jerry Suggs, Richard and Liz Reese…you and the McGowens are who I think of when I think of life-giving relationships. Your friendship is woven throughout this book and I can't thank you enough for all that you have done for me along the way.

Patrick and Cheryl, for so long you have joined Meeka and me on wild adventures! We are so thankful for your friendship and the example you are in following God on this grand adventure! Patrick, thanks for the picture that appears on the cover! I still remember that day!

Serving as a pastor, you get a front-row view of God's work in and through so many beautiful people. Most recently, I learned so much as I served at CyFair Christian Church and Christ Church Kingwood, where much of this material was developed. Thank you for being patient with me as God was at work in me while I was with you!

I'm thankful for the current board of directors as well as past directors at BetterDays. And, I'm especially thankful for Dianna Jonns and her constant support and behind the scenes help for so many years now.

As I start this new journey at Porter's Call in Franklin, Tennessee, I'm filled with great expectations and grateful to work alongside Al Andrews, Beth Barcus, and Laura Bane. Thanks for inviting me to be part of this amazing work.

Last, but certainly not least, I appreciate the patience and long-suffering of the team at Lucid: John Fox, Casey Cease, Sammantha

Acknowledgments

Lengl, and Laurie Waller, for bringing us to the finish line!

Go Outside!

Notes

1. Thomas Merton, *No Man Is an Island* (New York: Harcourt, 1955), 33.

2. N.T. Wright, *The Challenge of Jesus: Rediscovering Who Jesus Was and Is* (London, UK: IVP Books, 1999), 183. Bishop Wright mentions these three categories and says that we are made for God, sex, and gardening!

3. Jürgen Moltmann, Nicholas Wolterstorff, and Ellen T. Charry, *A Passion for God's Reign*, edited by Miroslav Volf (Grand Rapids: William B. Eerdmans, 1998), 3.

4. Martin Buber, *I and Thou* (New York: Scribner and Sons, 1970), 14.

5. Cornelius Plantiga Jr., *Not the Way It's Supposed to Be: A Breviary of Sin* (Grand Rapids: Eerdman's, 1995), 197. Plantinga uses this word to describe the effects of sin and I have always found this to be so helpful.

6. I first published this story in the book on marriage I coauthored, *To Become One* (Relevant, 2004)

7. Frederick Buechner, *Wishful Thinking: A Seeker's ABC* (New York: HarperCollins, 1993), 108.

8. Annie Dillard, *Pilgrim at Tinker Creek* (New York: Harper & Row Publishers, 1974), 15.

9. Thomas Merton, *No Man Is an Island* (New York: Harcourt, 1955), 33.

10. C.S. Lewis, *The Weight of Glory and Other Addresses* (San Francisco: HarperOne, 1980), 35.

11. G.K. Chesterton, *Orthodoxy* (San Francisco: Ignatius Press, 1908), 86.

www.ingramcontent.com/pod-product-compliance
Lightning Source LLC
Chambersburg PA
CBHW070205100426
42743CB00013B/3056